P9-CFY-676

DISCARDED

1st EDITION

Perspectives on Diseases and Disorders

Stroke

Arthur Gillard
Book Editor

Fitchburg Public Library
5530 Lacy Road
Fitchburg, WI 53711

WITHDRAWN

PERSPECTIVES
On Diseases & Disorders

GALE
CENGAGE Learning·

Detroit • New York • San Francisco • New Haven, Conn • Waterville, Maine • London

GALE
CENGAGE Learning·

Elizabeth Des Chenes, *Director, Publishing Solutions*

© 2013 Greenhaven Press, a part of Gale, Cengage Learning

Gale and Greenhaven Press are registered trademarks used herein under license.

For more information, contact:
Greenhaven Press
27500 Drake Rd.
Farmington Hills, MI 48331-3535
Or you can visit our Internet site at gale.cengage.com

ALL RIGHTS RESERVED.
No part of this work covered by the copyright herein may be reproduced, transmitted, stored, or used in any form or by any means graphic, electronic, or mechanical, including but not limited to photocopying, recording, scanning, digitizing, taping, Web distribution, information networks, or information storage and retrieval systems, except as permitted under Section 107 or 108 of the 1976 United States Copyright Act, without the prior written permission of the publisher.

For product information and technology assistance, contact us at

Gale Customer Support, 1-800-877-4253
For permission to use material from this text or product, submit all requests online at www.cengage.com/permissions

Further permissions questions can be e-mailed to permissionrequest@cengage.com

Articles in Greenhaven Press anthologies are often edited for length to meet page requirements. In addition, original titles of these works are changed to clearly present the main thesis and to explicitly indicate the author's opinion. Every effort is made to ensure that Greenhaven Press accurately reflects the original intent of the authors. Every effort has been made to trace the owners of copyrighted material.

Cover image © Deco Images II/Alamy

LIBRARY OF CONGRESS CATALOGING-IN-PUBLICATION DATA

Stroke / Arthur Gillard, book editor.
    p. cm. -- (Perspectives on diseases and disorders)
  Includes bibliographical references and index.
  ISBN 978-0-7377-6359-1 (hardcover)
  1. Cerebrovascular disease. 2. Cerebrovascular disease--Treatment. I. Gillard, Arthur.
  RC388.5.S8413 2012
  616.8'1--dc23

                                                                    2012019752

Printed in the United States of America
1 2 3 4 5 6 7 16 15 14 13 12

CONTENTS

CHAPTER 2   Controversies Surrounding Stroke

FOREWORD

"Medicine, to produce health, has to examine disease."
—Plutarch

Independent research on a health issue is often the first step to complement discussions with a physician. But locating accurate, well-organized, understandable medical information can be a challenge. A simple Internet search on terms such as "cancer" or "diabetes," for example, returns an intimidating number of results. Sifting through the results can be daunting, particularly when some of the information is inconsistent or even contradictory. The Greenhaven Press series Perspectives on Diseases and Disorders offers a solution to the often overwhelming nature of researching diseases and disorders.

From the clinical to the personal, titles in the Perspectives on Diseases and Disorders series provide students and other researchers with authoritative, accessible information in unique anthologies that include basic information about the disease or disorder, controversial aspects of diagnosis and treatment, and first-person accounts of those impacted by the disease. The result is a well-rounded combination of primary and secondary sources that, together, provide the reader with a better understanding of the disease or disorder.

Each volume in Perspectives on Diseases and Disorders explores a particular disease or disorder in detail. Material for each volume is carefully selected from a wide range of sources, including encyclopedias, journals, newspapers, nonfiction books, speeches, government documents, pamphlets, organization newsletters, and position papers. Articles in the first chapter provide an authoritative, up-to-date overview that covers symptoms, causes and effects, treatments, cures, and medical advances. The second chapter presents a substantial number of opposing viewpoints on controversial treatments and other current debates relating to the volume topic. The third chapter offers a variety of personal perspectives on the disease or disorder. Patients, doctors, caregivers, and loved ones represent just some of the voices found in this narrative chapter.

Each Perspectives on Diseases and Disorders volume also includes:

- An **annotated table of contents** that provides a brief summary of each article in the volume.

- An **introduction** specific to the volume topic.

- Full-color **charts and graphs** to illustrate key points, concepts, and theories.

- Full-color **photos** that show aspects of the disease or disorder and enhance textual material.

- **"Fast Facts"** that highlight pertinent additional statistics and surprising points.

- A **glossary** providing users with definitions of important terms.

- A **chronology** of important dates relating to the disease or disorder.

- An annotated list of **organizations to contact** for students and other readers seeking additional information.

- A **bibliography** of additional books and periodicals for further research.

- A detailed **subject index** that allows readers to quickly find the information they need.

Whether a student researching a disorder, a patient recently diagnosed with a disease, or an individual who simply wants to learn more about a particular disease or disorder, a reader who turns to Perspectives on Diseases and Disorders will find a wealth of information in each volume that offers not only basic information, but also vigorous debate from multiple perspectives.

INTRODUCTION

S troke is a devastating illness that often strikes without warning. An interruption of the blood supply to a region of the brain, caused either by a blockage or a rupture in a blood vessel, causes a sudden loss of brain function. Depending on which area(s) of the brain are deprived of the vital nutrients and oxygen contained in the blood, stroke can manifest in a myriad of different ways. Many people in the United States are living lives that have been radically altered by stroke. In the past most strokes were fatal, but due to medical advances over the past several decades, many people now survive strokes. And as scientists learn more about the brain, better treatments and rehabilitation techniques are being developed all the time.

Patricia H., an amateur painter and the curator of an art gallery, had a severe stroke that put her into a coma for at least twenty hours before she was discovered. On examination, she was found to have a massive blood clot in her left hemisphere and was not expected to live. Following surgery to remove the clot, Patricia was barely conscious of her surroundings. One of Patricia's daughters recalled how she would "stare . . . without seeming to see. Sometimes her eyes would follow me, or seem to. We didn't know what was going on, whether she was there."[1] After two weeks she emerged from this minimally conscious state with her personality intact and showing awareness of her environment. However, the stroke had caused serious damage: The right side of Patricia's body was totally paralyzed, and she had aphasia—a communications disorder caused by damage to the language centers in her left hemisphere. She had little or no ability to understand speech and could only communicate her feelings and thoughts through gestures. For a vivacious, extroverted person like Patricia, the loss of language was much more devastating than the paralysis of the right side of her body. As Oliver Sacks, a neurologist who studied her case, noted, "I would sometimes see her, in this first year after her stroke, sitting alone in the corridor or in the patients' dayroom, bereft of speech . . . with a stricken and desolate look on her face."[2] Patricia's daughters were given a very discouraging prognosis, according to Sacks: "A little improvement . . . might occur, but Pat would need to be put away for the rest of her life; there would be no parties, no conversation, no art galleries anymore—all that had constituted the very essence of Pat's life would be gone, and she would lead the narrow life of a patient, an inmate, in an institution."[3]

Howard Engel, a Canadian writer of detective novels, had a very different experience with stroke. His day started out normally, but when he attempted to read his morning newspaper, he was surprised to find that he could no longer understand the words—all the letters "looked like Cyrillic [Eastern European alphabet] one moment and Korean the next,"[4] he recalls. At first he thought friends had played a practical joke on him, but he soon realized he must have had a stroke. Hospital tests confirmed his suspicion, and it became clear that in addition to his sudden alexia (inability to read), he had other symptoms as well: a large blind spot in his visual field, reduced short-term memory, and transient difficulties recognizing faces, colors, and commonplace objects. As he explains, "Familiar objects like apples and oranges suddenly look[ed] strange, as unfamiliar as an exotic piece of Asian fruit. . . . I would surprise myself with not knowing whether I was holding an orange or a grapefruit, a tomato or an apple. Usually, I could sort them out by sniffing or squeezing."[5] Although his symptoms were relatively mild, his sudden inability to read was extremely challenging for a man who strongly identified as a reader and who made his living as

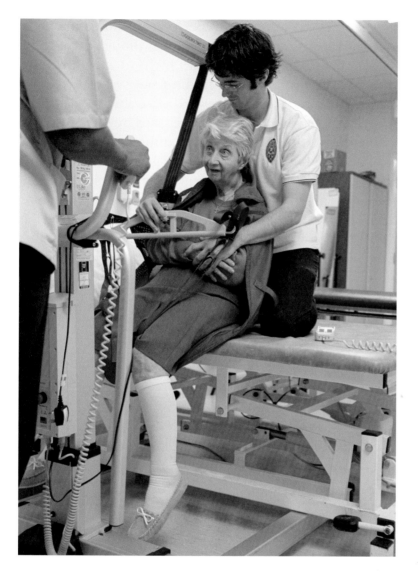

A stroke victim undergoes physical therapy. A stroke is a devastating cardiovascular disease that often strikes without warning and can manifest itself in a number of different ways. (© **Tom Stoddart/ Getty Images**)

an author. Howard wondered how he could possibly cope with his new condition.

More and more, scientists are discovering that the brain is much more adaptable than was once believed. The burgeoning field of neuroplasticity has shown that the brain is continually forming new circuits—even after a catastrophic insult such as a stroke—recruiting surviving neurons to take over lost or impaired functions when the neurons that originally performed those functions are damaged or destroyed. And even though significant deficits may remain, people can learn to accommodate their reduced abilities by finding new ways of doing things. Both Patricia and Howard were able to adapt to a surprising degree to the damage caused by their strokes.

Howard soon discovered that although he could not read anymore, he could still write; because reading and writing are controlled by different brain areas, it is possible to lose one ability but not the other. He learned to recognize letters by tracing them out with his fingers—recruiting the part of his brain that could still write in order to comprehend text, essentially "reading by writing." Sacks explains:

> Increasingly and often unconsciously . . . Howard started to move his hands as he read, tracing the outlines of words and sentences still unintelligible to his eyes. And most remarkably, his tongue, too, began to move as he read, tracing the shapes of letters on his teeth or the roof of his mouth. This enabled him to read considerably faster. . . . Thus, by an extraordinary . . . sensory-motor alchemy, Howard was replacing reading by a sort of writing. He was, in effect, reading with his tongue.[6]

Although still alexic, Howard was able to sufficiently adapt to, and overcome, his reduced abilities to resume his career as a writer; only a few years after his stroke, he wrote a new detective novel, *Memory Book*, based on his experiences of stroke, followed by a memoir detailing his illness and recovery, *The Man Who Forgot How to Read*.

Patricia's stroke was much more serious, involving as it did an almost complete loss of language and total paralysis of the right side of her body. As with many of those affected by aphasia, although her mind and personality were largely intact, she felt isolated, unable to connect with others. As time went on, however, Patricia developed a remarkable ability to discern the intentions and emotions of other people and to communicate via gesture and mime—a type of compensation often experienced by aphasic stroke patients. A further breakthrough came when it was discovered that Patricia could recognize individual written words. Patricia's speech pathologist provided her with a lexicon, or list, of common words organized into categories such as moods, people, and events. Between her heightened powers of gestural communication and the lexicon, Patricia was able to resume a vibrant social life again.

Someone who has a stroke will never be the same as he or she was before. He or she will face new challenges and reduced abilities. Despite this, it is possible to move forward and to live a rich and meaningful life. As the spiritual teacher Ram Dass, who himself suffered a severe stroke, observed, "I've learned that the fear of something like stroke is often worse than the thing itself. The stroke is a terrible grace, but I've learned that it is a grace that the soul can use . . . the stroke taught me . . . how clinging to the past leads to suffering."[7]

Perspectives on Diseases and Disorders: Stroke provides an accessible overview of a challenging disease. Incorporating the perspectives of experts, health care providers, and stroke sufferers themselves, this volume provides opportunities to enhance awareness about one of the most common and serious medical conditions.

Notes

1. Quoted in Oliver Sacks, *The Mind's Eye.* New York: Knopf, 2010, p. 33.
2. Sacks, *The Mind's Eye*, p. 41.
3. Sacks, *The Mind's Eye*, p. 38.
4. Quoted in Sacks, *The Mind's Eye*, p. 53.
5. Quoted in Sacks, *The Mind's Eye*, p. 55.
6. Sacks, *The Mind's Eye*, pp. 77–78.
7. Quoted in Sounds True, "When Is a Life-Threatening Stroke a Form of 'Grace'—with Ram Dass." www .soundstrue.com/articles/When_is_a_life-threatening _stroke_a_form_of_grace-with_Ram_Dass.

CHAPTER 1

Understanding Stroke

An Overview of Stroke

Evelyn B. Kelly

Evelyn B. Kelly is a writer and public speaker. She is the author of *Health and Medical Issues Today: Stem Cells* and contributed one hundred articles to *Science and Its Times: A Seven Volume Encyclopedia on the History of Medicine*. In the following viewpoint Kelly distinguishes between two main types of stroke: ischemic stroke, which occurs when an artery is blocked and results in a decrease or cessation of blood flow to the brain; and hemorrhagic stroke, which occurs when an artery in the brain ruptures, flooding the surrounding tissue with blood. According to the author, a stroke may be accompanied by various symptoms such as nausea, numbness, paralysis, and loss of coordination. She says that onset of symptoms is typically sudden, and the exact symptoms will depend on which part of the brain is affected. Kelly describes a number of risk factors, such as high blood pressure, obesity, and sleep disorders.

Photo on facing page. A stroke patient has his cardiac functions monitored to help doctors better understand his cardiovascular status. (© Antonia Reeve/Photo Researchers, Inc.)

SOURCE: Evelyn B. Kelly, "Stroke and Related Disorders," *Diseases and Disorders,* vol. 3, 2008. Copyright © 2008 by Marshall Cavendish. All rights reserved. Reproduced by permission.

The medical term for stroke is *cerebrovascular disease*, and it is sometimes referred to as a cerebrovascular accident, or CVA. The word *cerebrovascular* comes from the Latin word *cerebro*, which means "brain," and *vasa* which means "vessel."

The brain requires about 20 percent of the heart's output of fresh blood to supply its requirements for oxygen and glucose. Two artery systems, the carotid arteries, carry blood through the neck to the brain. Anything that disturbs the blood flow, even for a few seconds, affects the brain's function. Depending on the area of the brain, a variety of the following symptoms may occur: sudden numbness, weakness, or paralysis on one side of the body, such as the face, arm, or leg; sudden nausea, fever, or vomiting; sudden difficulty speaking or understanding speech (aphasia); sudden blurred vision, double vision, or decreased vision in one or both eyes; sudden dizziness, loss of balance, or loss of coordination; sudden loss of consciousness; sudden confusion or memory problems, loss of spatial orientation or perception; sudden headache, as a bolt out of the blue. The key word for each of these symptoms is sudden. There will frequently be more than one sign. Any of these symptoms signal a medical emergency. Every minute the brain cells are deprived of oxygen increases the risk of damage. Chances for recovery are much better when the right treatment is begun within the first few hours of noticing stroke symptoms.

Two major types of cerebrovascular events are ischemic stroke, in which blood does not get to part of the brain due to a disturbance in blood flow; and cerebral hemorrhage, during which blood vessels in the brain bleed and the released (hemorrhagic) blood damages brain tissue. The term *stroke* is commonly applied to the clinical symptoms and not to a specific condition.

Ischemic Stroke

The word *ischemia* literally means "to hold back blood." This type of stroke occurs when an artery suddenly becomes blocked and decreases or stops the flow of blood to the brain. Cells may begin to die within minutes. This type is responsible for 80 percent of all strokes. There are two conditions that cause this type of stroke. The first is embolic stroke, which is a type of ischemia, in which a clot forms in another part of the body, travels through blood vessels, and becomes wedged in a brain artery. The free-roaming clot or embolus often forms in the heart. The type of clot is often caused by irregular beating in the two upper chambers of the heart. This irregular beating is called atrial fibrillation, which leads to poor blood flow and the formation of a clot.

The two types of stroke are illustrated here. A hemorrhagic stroke is depicted on the left, in which blood leaks into the brain tissue. In an ischemic stroke (right), a clot or other blockage stops blood flow to the brain. (© **Nucleus Medical Art, Inc./Alamy**)

The second type is thrombotic stroke, in which a blood clot forms in one of the cerebral arteries and grows until it is large enough to block the blood flow. Buildup of

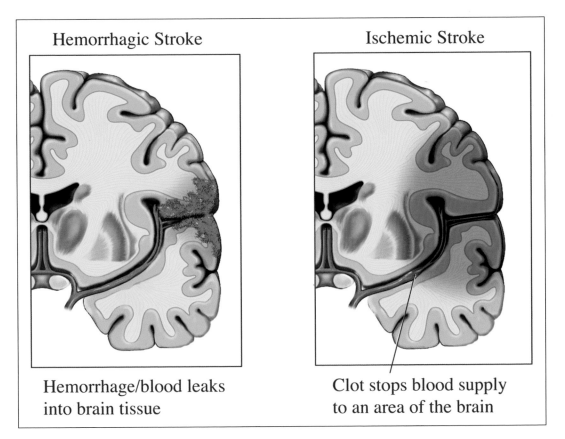

Hemorrhagic Stroke

Ischemic Stroke

Hemorrhage/blood leaks into brain tissue

Clot stops blood supply to an area of the brain

plaques (a mixture of fatty substances including choles-terol and other lipids) causes stenosis or narrowing of the artery as a result of these fatty deposits in the artery wall. When a stroke occurs as a result of small vessel disease, an infarction occurs. An infarction is the deprivation of blood supply of part of a tissue or organ in which an area of dead tissue (infarct) forms. Infarcted tissue swells and becomes firm, blood vessels around the infarct widen, and plasma and blood may flow into the infarct, thus increasing the swelling. The infarct then shrinks and is replaced by fibrous scar tis-sue, and function is lost.

> **FAST FACT**
>
> According to the Centers for Disease Control and Prevention, every forty seconds someone in the United States has a stroke, and every four minutes a fatal stroke occurs.

Transient ischemic attacks (TIAs) may in-dicate that a stroke is coming. These are minor attacks in which the person may have a sudden onset of weakness, vertigo, or imbalance, that lasts only a few minutes. These attacks have the same origin as ischemic stroke. Attacks are probably due to atherosclerosis, when plaque fragments break off and travel to a site in the brain. Major risk factors are high blood pres-sure, smoking, diabetes, and advanced age. The most significant factor is that the symptoms and signs last no more than 24 hours. If the symptom recurs, it often is a warning that a stroke may follow. One of the most com-mon treatments for this condition is aspirin. Aspirin inhibits the way in which platelets clump together. Too many platelets gathered in a constricted area may block the flow to the brain.

Hemorrhagic Stroke

Hemorrhage is the medical word for bleeding. A hemor-rhagic stroke occurs when an artery in the brain bursts, sending blood into surrounding tissue. Symptoms in-clude severe headache, drowsiness, seizures, or confu-sion after a head injury, paralysis on one side of the body, or changes in personality. This type of stroke accounts for about 20 percent of all strokes and happens in two ways. First, it can happen as an aneurysm; a thin or weak spot on the artery wall balloons out and ruptures, spilling blood into spaces surrounding the brain tissue. The ruptured brain arteries bleed into the brain itself or into spaces surrounding the brain.

Second, the stroke can occur as an intracerebral hemorrhage, when the vessel in the brain leaks blood into the brain itself. In this case, brain cells beyond the leak are deprived of blood and are also damaged.

High blood pressure is the most common cause of hemorrhagic stroke. High blood pressure causes small arteries in the brain to become stiff and subject to cracking or rupture. A subarachnoid hemorrhage is bleeding under the meninges into the outer covering of the brain, which contaminates the cerebrospinal fluid (CSF). Because the CSF circulates through the cranium, this type of stroke can lead to extensive damage and is the most deadly of all strokes. . . .

Risk Factors

Several red flags for stroke include hypertension, hyperlipidemia, obesity, sleep disorders, homocysteine levels, and certain lifestyle behaviors. The chance of risk is slightly higher if one of the parents or brother or sister has had a stroke or TIA; age is also a risk factor. High blood pressure (HBP), also called hypertension, is highly correlated to stroke. . . . People who have abdominal fat (apple shapes) tend to have elevated blood pressure. For example, obese adults ages 20 to 45 are six times more likely to have high blood pressure than normal adults of the same age. Obese people who are 20 percent above standard weight show a 10 percent risk of stroke. . . .

Hyperlipidemia or elevated levels of serum triglycerides (fats) are linked to stroke. Healthy arteries have a thin and smooth inner surface that allows blood to flow freely to deliver oxygen to the cells, including the 20 percent payload that the brain demands. In a diseased artery, the inner layer consists of a pool of fat that becomes covered with a hard crust called plaque, which forms inside the artery. Smooth muscle cells migrate to the built-up area, and a small crack appears in the lining, where a blood clot forms. The buildup can be in any artery in the body, including the carotid artery in the neck that leads to the brain. As the abnormal deposits of fats and cholesterol grow and develop, the internal bore (lumen) of the artery gets narrower and narrower. Also, some of the plaque may break away and circulate in the bloodstream to the brain. According to several studies, TIA strokes appear closely related to hyperlipidemia.

People who sleep more than eight hours a night, who snore, or who experience daytime drowsiness have increased risk for stroke. Obstructive sleep apnea (OSA) is a sleep disorder characterized by episodes of not breathing, called apnea. This condition results from a collapse of the upper airway at the area of the back of the throat called the pharnyx. During an episode of apnea, the person tries to breathe against the closed airway, but he or she is not getting oxygen, and a condition called hypoxia occurs. The brain senses the lack of oxygen, and the person wakes up briefly to restore the upper-airway passage. The cycle may be repeated a hundred times during the night, disrupting normal sleep. The person rarely remembers. OSA can lead to stroke by reducing the amount of oxygen that reaches the brain.

Several lifestyle behavioral factors correlate with stroke. One study found that 28 percent of strokes follow alcohol use and 8 percent after heavy exertion. Other examples were lifting more than 50 pounds, 10 percent; straining during urination or defecation, 4 percent; anger outbursts, 4 percent; and sexual intercourse, 2 percent. Another lifestyle condition is metabolic syndrome, or Syndrome X, in which a cluster of major risk factors of life habits such as alcohol abuse, improper nutrition, inadequate physical activity, and increased body weight

Ischemic and Hemorrhagic Stroke

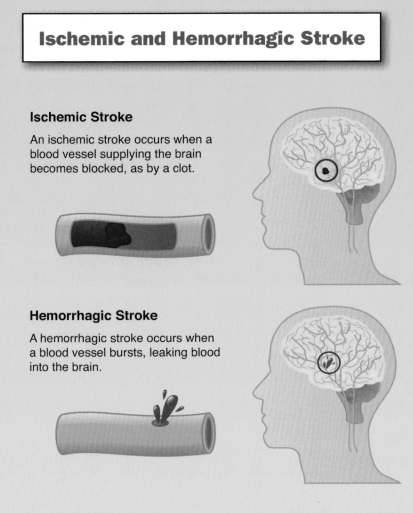

Ischemic Stroke

An ischemic stroke occurs when a blood vessel supplying the brain becomes blocked, as by a clot.

Hemorrhagic Stroke

A hemorrhagic stroke occurs when a blood vessel bursts, leaking blood into the brain.

Taken from: "Stroke: Challenges, Progress, and Promise: Introduction." National Institute of Neurological Disorders and Stroke. http://stroke, http://stroke.nih.gov/materials/strokechallenges.htm.

all converge to create cardiovascular problems and risk of stroke. Other factors include gender (women tend to die more with strokes), cigarette smoking, diabetes, use of birth control bills, and hormone therapy.

Certain medications have been related to stroke. In October 2000 the U.S. Food and Drug Administration (FDA) removed phenylpropanolamine (PPA) from over 400 over-the-counter cold, cough, and some diet medications. The FDA found PPA caused 200 to 500 strokes in people under 50, who were mostly women.

Epidemiology

Accurate reporting techniques are being developed and refined. A 2001 study reported that rates of the first ischemic stroke, intracerebral hemorrhage, and subarachnoid hemorrhage were 25 to 50 percent higher among people of African American descent than among Caucasians. The study found that the general U.S. population will suffer 760,000 strokes each year, and more than 11 million suffer silent strokes or TIAs. Historically, the Southeast, especially Alabama and Mississippi, has been referred to as the stroke belt because the area had more strokes than other sections of the country. However, there are indications that the western states of Oregon, Washington, and Arizona may, in the future, have the highest incidence of strokes.

Figures from the National Stroke Foundation have revealed a startling number of young adults who have had strokes. About 225,000 Americans under the age of 45, including young and middle-aged women, have had strokes. One stroke victim of a brain aneurysm was 13; she was fortunate the aneurysm had only ballooned out, and it was caught before it burst. Drug abuse has led to 85 to 90 percent of hemorrhagic strokes occurring in people in their 20s and 30s. In 2002 around 275,000 people in the United States died after having a stroke; stroke accounted for 1 in 15 deaths in the United States. Stroke is the third leading cause of death after heart disease and cancer.

Diagnosing and Treating Stroke

National Institute of Neurological Disorders and Stroke

The National Institute of Neurological Disorders and Stroke (NINDS) is a division of the National Institutes of Health (NIH) tasked with reducing the burden of neurological disease, including stroke. In the following viewpoint the author describes stroke diagnosis using methods such as the NIH Stroke Scale, used by physicians to assess a patient's symptoms, as well as a number of brain imaging techniques, including computed tomography (CT) and magnetic resonance imaging (MRI). NINDS also provides an extensive overview of stroke treatment and preventive measures using medication and surgery. For example, tissue plasminogen activator (tPA) is a drug that helps restore blood flow after ischemic stroke, thus reducing brain injury, but can only be used safely under certain circumstances. NINDS also discusses the important role of rehabilitation, noting that the brain's plasticity (ability to reorganize by making new connections between brain cells) enables patients to relearn lost skills.

SOURCE: *Stroke: Challenges, Progress, and Promise, NIH Publication No. 09-6451*, National Institute of Neurological Disorders and Stroke (NINDS), February 2009, www.ninds.nih.gov. Copyright © 2009 by National Institute of Neurological Disorders and Stroke.

When a stroke is suspected, a physician will carry out a detailed assessment of the individual's signs and symptoms. One common assessment tool is the NIH [National Institutes of Health] Stroke Scale, developed by NINDS [National Institute of Neurological Disorders and Stroke]. This is a checklist of questions and tasks that scores an individual's level of alertness and ability to communicate and perform simple movements. Other common diagnostic procedures include blood tests and an electrocardiogram to check for cardiac abnormalities that might have contributed to the stroke.

Stroke Diagnostics and Brain Imaging

Brain imaging techniques play an important role in stroke diagnosis, in the evaluation of individuals with stroke for clinical trials, and, to a growing extent, assessment of stroke risk. Several imaging techniques can be used to generate visual "slices" of the brain or even three-dimensional reconstructions. This in-depth look at the brain helps to: rule out other potential neurological conditions such as a brain tumor, differentiate ischemic from hemorrhagic stroke, identify which blood vessels have been damaged, and determine the extent and location of the infarct [a small area of dead tissue caused by a loss of blood supply].

Computed tomography (CT) and magnetic resonance imaging (MRI) are the two most common imaging techniques used to identify infarctions caused by stroke. CT uses X-ray beams passed through the head at multiple angles to generate high-resolution brain images. It is faster, more widely available, and less expensive than MRI.

MRI, which does not involve X-rays, exposes the brain to a magnetic field in combination with a radio wave pulse. The brain's absorption of this pulse and the rate at which energy is released when the pulse ends varies in different brain tissues and yields an image. Diffusion-weighted imaging (DWI) is a highly sensitive type of MRI that measures the diffusion of water in brain tissue, which changes during an ischemic stroke. DWI is especially useful for detecting small infarcts and is superior to CT for diagnosing ischemic stroke. Research studies suggest that DWI in combination with a brain blood perfusion [measuring the rate of blood flow] study can be used to help identify the ischemic penumbra—brain tissue that is blood-starved, but salvageable if blood flow can be restored quickly. In many individuals, the extent of ischemic penumbra is related to the degree of diffusion-perfusion mismatch, which is a DWI signal that occurs in brain tissue with normal water diffusion but abnormal blood flow.

Several imaging techniques are used to examine cerebral blood vessels. These techniques can reveal the site of blockage in an ischemic stroke or detect stenosis or vascular malformations (such as an aneurysm or AVM [arteriovenous malformation]) that put a person at risk for stroke. Angiography of the brain involves imaging after a contrast agent that shows up dark on a scan has been injected into a vein in the arm or leg, which yields a map of the brain's blood vessels.

A procedurally similar technique called perfusion imaging is sensitive for detecting abnormal blood flow in the brain. Doppler ultrasound involves passing high-frequency, inaudible sound waves into the neck or head. These sound waves bounce off of cells moving through the blood, producing an image and providing information on how fast the blood is traveling. In general, blood cells speed up as they move through a narrow vessel. . . .

Current Stroke Treatment and Prevention

Today, there is a small but growing arsenal of treatments that can markedly improve the chances of recovering from a stroke. There is also a wealth of knowledge about what causes stroke and how to reduce the chances of having one. . . .

Thrombolytic Drugs, Antiplatelet Drugs, and Anticoagulants

In treating acute ischemic stroke (acute meaning that the stroke has occurred within the past few hours), the immediate goal is to break apart the offending clot, a process known as thrombolysis. The body produces its own thrombolytic proteins, and some of these have been engineered into drugs. One, called tissue plasminogen activator (tPA), had a proven track record for treating heart attacks. In the late 1980s, NINDS-funded investigators laid the plans for the first placebo-controlled trial of tPA to treat acute ischemic stroke. They knew from animal studies that irreversible brain injury is likely to occur if blood flow is not restored within the first few hours after ischemic stroke. Therefore, the NINDS tPA Study Group tested the drug within a three-hour time window. Compared to individuals given placebo, those given intravenous tPA were more likely to have minimal or no disability three months after treatment—a finding that persuaded the U.S. Food and Drug Administration to approve tPA for use against acute stroke. . . .

Because treatment with tPA interferes with blood clotting and has also been shown to increase leaking along the blood-brain barrier, it carries a risk of intracerebral hemorrhage. Therefore, it is not recommended for some people, such as those with a history of brain hemorrhage or significantly elevated blood pressure. The risk of tPA-induced hemorrhage increases over time from stroke onset, which has limited its use to the first three hours after stroke (where benefit was most clearly established in the U.S. trials).

Blood-thinning medications fall into two classes: antiplatelet drugs and anticoagulants. Antiplatelet drugs inhibit the activity of cells called platelets, which stick to damaged areas inside blood vessels and lay the foundation for blood clots. The most common antiplatelet drug is aspirin. Anticoagulants, such as heparin (produced by

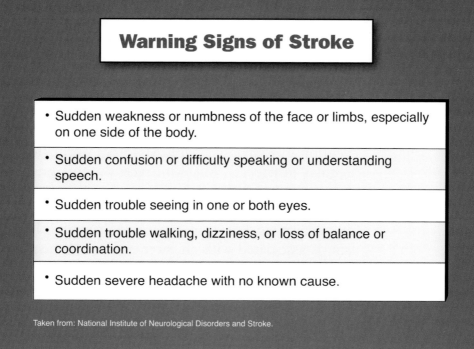

Warning Signs of Stroke

- Sudden weakness or numbness of the face or limbs, especially on one side of the body.
- Sudden confusion or difficulty speaking or understanding speech.
- Sudden trouble seeing in one or both eyes.
- Sudden trouble walking, dizziness, or loss of balance or coordination.
- Sudden severe headache with no known cause.

Taken from: National Institute of Neurological Disorders and Stroke.

inflammatory cells in the body) and warfarin (found in plants and also known by the trade name Coumadin©), inhibit proteins in the blood that stimulate clotting.

Ongoing Research

Antiplatelet drugs and anticoagulants can help prevent a variety of potentially life-threatening conditions for which individuals with stroke are at risk, such as myocardial infarction, pulmonary embolism, and deep vein thrombosis—which are caused by clots in the heart, lungs and deep veins of the legs, respectively. In recent years, the value of these drugs in treating and preventing stroke itself has been more closely scrutinized.

One focus of this research has been to determine if there is any benefit in giving antiplatelet drugs or anticoagulants during an acute ischemic stroke, as an adjunct to tPA, or as an alternative for people ineligible to receive tPA. In an international trial . . . aspirin significantly reduced the risk of a recurrent ischemic stroke at two weeks. A similar benefit from heparin was offset by an increased risk of hemorrhagic stroke. . . .

Another issue is whether individuals at risk for ischemic stroke should be placed on a daily maintenance program of aspirin or anticoagulants. For many years, aspirin and warfarin were used as a means of stroke prevention in individuals with AF [atrial fibrillation, an irregular heartbeat], but until recently, this practice was based more on anecdotal evidence than on scientific data. A systematic analysis of warfarin's benefits was especially important since it is an expensive drug and, like heparin, is associated with an increased risk of hemorrhagic stroke. The NINDS Boston Area Anticoagulation Trial for Atrial Fibrillation (BAATAF) and the Stroke Prevention in Atrial Fibrillation (SPAF) trials showed that daily warfarin is best for people with AF who are over age 65 or who have additional vascular risk factors. Daily aspirin provides adequate protection against stroke among young people with AF. . . .

Medication for Subarachnoid Hemorrhage

The drug nimodipine is used to treat cerebral vasospasm, a complication that sometimes follows subarachnoid hemorrhage. This refers to a constriction of blood vessels in the brain that can significantly reduce blood flow, leading to ischemia and infarction. Although its precise origins are unclear, cerebral vasospasm is thought to be triggered in part by an influx of calcium into the smooth muscles that control blood vessel diameter. Nimodipine is a calcium antagonist, meaning that it works by blocking the entry of calcium into cells. Nimodipine has been shown to reduce infarction and improve outcome in individuals with subarachnoid hemorrhage. . . .

Surgeries and Other Procedures

Surgery is sometimes used to clear the congested blood vessels that cause ischemic stroke or to repair the vascular abnormalities that contribute to hemorrhagic stroke.

A surgery called carotid endarterectomy involves removing plaque to widen the carotids, a pair of arteries that ascend each side of the neck and are the main suppliers of blood to the brain. Stenosis that narrows a carotid artery by more than 50 percent is considered clinically significant. In some cases, carotid stenosis is first detected after a person experiences a stroke or other symptoms, such as a TIA [transient ischemic attack]. It is also sometimes detected in the absence of symptoms, as when a physician presses a stethoscope to the neck and hears a bruit—a sound made by blood flowing past an obstruction. The presence of carotid stenosis can be confirmed by angiography or Doppler ultrasound.

Data from NINDS-funded research show that the risk of ischemic stroke from clinically significant asymptomatic carotid stenosis is about two to three percent per year (meaning that out of 100 individuals with this condition, two or three will have a stroke each year). The risk of ischemic stroke from clinically significant symptomatic carotid stenosis is much higher—about 25 percent during the first two years following the appearance of symptoms. . . .

Endarterectomy itself is associated with a small risk of stroke because the disruption of plaque during the procedure can send emboli [circulating particles] into the bloodstream, or cause a clot at the site of surgery. NINDS supports the investigation of an alternative procedure known as carotid artery stenting, which involves inserting a stent (a tube-like device that is made of mesh-like material) into the carotid artery. The stent is compressed until the radiologist threads it into position, and is then expanded to mechanically widen the artery. It is also equipped with a downstream "umbrella" to catch dislodged plaque. . . .

> **FAST FACT**
>
> The *New England Journal of Medicine* reported in 2011 that patients treated with stenting to prevent stroke fared significantly worse than those given intensive medical intervention to control risk factors.

Several techniques are used to eliminate the vascular abnormalities linked to hemorrhagic stroke, or at least to reduce the risk that they will rupture. Arteriovenous malformations (AVMs) can be surgically removed through a procedure known as surgical resection. They can also be treated non-invasively (without the need to cut into the skull) using radiosurgery or embolization. Radiosurgery involves directing a beam of radiation at the AVM, while embolization involves injecting artificial emboli (usually made of foam) into the AVM to block it off from its parent vessel.

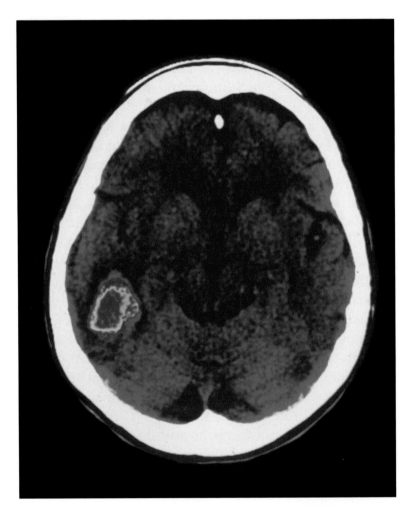

A computed tomography (CT) scan of a woman's brain shows a hemorrhage in the left posterior temporal area of the brain (in red). (© Scott Camazine/Alamy Images)

Clipping and coiling are procedures used to treat intracerebral aneurysms. Clipping involves opening the skull and placing a clip near the aneurysm, to separate it from its parent blood vessel. In endovascular coiling, a wire topped with a detachable coil is inserted into a leg artery and threaded into the aneurysm. Once in place, the coil is released into the aneurysm, where it stimulates blood clotting and strengthens the blood vessel wall. Stents are also used in some cases to divert blood flow away from an aneurysm. . . .

Rehabilitation

Stroke rehabilitation includes physical therapy and other approaches intended to help individuals achieve long-term recovery from stroke. Physical therapy involves using exercises to restore movement and coordination. Many people also receive occupational therapy, which focuses on improving daily activities such as eating, drinking, dressing, bathing, reading, and writing. Speech therapy may help people who have problems producing or understanding speech. Finally, since depression, anxiety, and social isolation are common among individuals who have had a stroke, the potential benefits of psychological or psychiatric treatment should be considered.

Importantly, the goal of rehabilitation is not simply for the individual to cope with disability, but to relearn skills that have been lost. This relearning is made possible by the brain's plasticity—its ability to reorganize itself by forming new connections between neurons. Plasticity soars in the developing brain and wanes as the brain matures, but even the aged brain appears to retain some plasticity and thus some capacity to repair itself after a stroke.

Basic research on the brain has shown that the most active neural connections tend to become stronger while the quietest connections tend to weaken until they disappear. Inspired by these findings, researchers are testing a few innovative techniques that follow a "use it or lose it" approach to stroke rehabilitation.

One technique, called constraint-induced movement therapy (CIMT), focuses on improving upper limb function in people with stroke who are affected by hemiparesis (weakening on one side of the body). It involves constant restraint of the unaffected hand and arm with a mitt shaped like a boxing glove, so that the person is forced to use the affected hand and arm for daily activities. Meanwhile, the person receives regular training sessions to exercise the weakened arm. . . .

Another technique involves using a body-weight-supported treadmill (BWST) to help people who have trouble walking. Individuals walk on a treadmill while being supported by an overhead harness, which protects them from falling and allows them to concentrate on coordination and speed. Recently, investigators have begun to combine BWST training with "overground" training, where individuals immediately practice what they have learned on the treadmill by walking with assistance and encouragement from a physical therapist. . . .

Scientists continue to investigate ways to better understand, diagnose, and treat stroke. Much of this research is conducted by the stroke community at the NIH or through research grants to academic centers throughout the United States.

Perceptual and Other Impairments Caused by Stroke

Kip Burkman

Kip Burkman is a physical medicine and rehabilitation physician at Alegent Health Immanuel Rehabilitation Center in Omaha, Nebraska. In the following viewpoint Burkman describes changes in perception, intellect, behavior, and emotions that may result from a stroke. According to the author, touch and vision are the senses most commonly damaged by stroke. Changes to vision can include blind spots, double vision, or even cortical blindness, a condition in which the patient loses the ability to process visual information. In one variation known as Anton's syndrome, the patient may not even realize that he or she is blind. Damage to the sense of touch may result in an inability to perceive pain correctly or in a sensation of numbness. Burkman notes that the ability to learn and understand can be adversely affected by stroke, and the patient may also behave inappropriately or have poor emotional control.

SOURCE: Kip Burkman, *The Stroke Recovery Book,* Omaha NE: Addicus Books, 2010, pp. 14–20. Copyright © 2010 by Addicus Books. All rights reserved. Reproduced by permission.

The brain is a vastly complex organ. No one has solved all its mysteries and its amazing capabilities. However, we know the unique human ability to process information occurs in the outer layer of the brain called the cerebral cortex. Damage to these brain tissues can result in a number of changes in cognition, a term that refers to the process of thinking and knowing things. It includes awareness, reasoning, remembering, perception, and problem solving. A stroke can also affect sensation, or the senses—smell, sight, hearing, touch, and taste.

To better understand how stroke can affect cognition and sensation, let's examine four basic elements: perception, intellect, behavior, and emotions.

Perception

Perception refers to the way we perceive the world around us. Perception includes depth perception, spatial orientation, and balance. It also includes vision, hearing, taste, smell, and touch. Of all the senses, vision and touch are most often affected by stroke.

Strokes can affect vision in several ways. Blind spots may occur when blood clots travel to the back part of the eye and damage the retina. A patient with a blind spot from a right hemisphere stroke may not see a cup of coffee placed on the left side of a breakfast tray. If a blind spot lasts longer than one month after a stroke, it will likely remain a problem. Therapists and nurses teach patients to remember to turn their heads to scan the total environment using their residual vision. Many patients need continued reminders to use this compensatory technique.

Damage to other visual pathways in the brain can result in visual field cuts. This impairment can be likened to covering half the lenses of your eyeglasses with black paint so that a portion of vision is blocked. A patient with a visual field cut may trip over unseen obstacles. Patients with visual field cuts often have a gaze preference. They seem to look only in the direction of the vision that remains.

Double vision, or diplopia may result when a stroke affects the brain stem. Some cranial nerves coming out of the brain stem control muscles that move the eyes. If one or more of these nerves is injured, the eyes are not able to move together. This produces two somewhat overlapping images that the brain interprets as double vision. To make only one image reach the brain, some patients will close one eye while others will wear an eye patch, alternated daily between the eyes.

Injury to both occipital lobes in the brain causes cortical blindness, a loss of the ability to interpret visual input. Some individuals may suffer total blindness, while others may be able to distinguish between light and dark. The most peculiar form of cortical blindness is Anton's syndrome, in which a patient is not aware that he is blind. The patient may even insist that all he needs is a pair of glasses to correct his vision.

Touch and Proprioception

Touch is the second sense most commonly affected by stroke. Strokes can cause the loss of touch sensation, pressure, vibration, and temperature—hot and cold.

Consider the complexity of the sense of touch. If you prick your finger on a pin, a nerve receptor sends a message to the thalamus, the brain's "relay" center. From there, the message is sent to the parietal lobe of the brain, and you receive the message that you've stuck your finger. Your reaction is to jerk your finger away from the source of the pain. The entire sequence occurs in an instant. However, a patient who has suffered injury to the parts of the brain responsible for touch sensation may be unaware that his finger was pricked.

Loss of touch sensation is commonly marked by numbness in the limbs. This makes various tasks more

Brain Areas That Can Be Damaged by Stroke

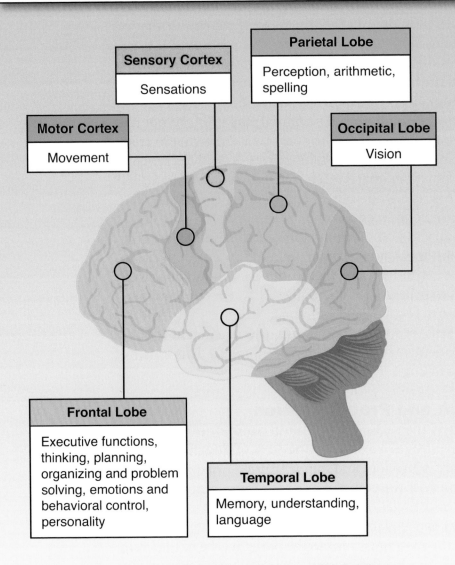

Sensory Cortex
Sensations

Parietal Lobe
Perception, arithmetic, spelling

Motor Cortex
Movement

Occipital Lobe
Vision

Frontal Lobe
Executive functions, thinking, planning, organizing and problem solving, emotions and behavioral control, personality

Temporal Lobe
Memory, understanding, language

Taken from: "About the Brain." The Brain Injury Association. www.headway.org.uk/About-the-brain.aspx.

difficult. For example, a patient with a numb hand may crush a paper cup when he picks it up because he can't feel the pressure he's applying. Inability to grasp also interferes with dressing, eating, brushing the hair or teeth, and walking with canes or walkers.

Joint position proprioception refers to knowing the position of your hand, arm, or leg in space or in relation to other objects. If this sense of joint position is lost, patients can't feel the position of limbs. This creates problems when walking, because patients can't tell when their feet hit the ground. Balance is affected because the ability to feel shifting weight is lost. These patients must learn to use their eyes to judge the relationship between their feet and the floor.

Intellect, Behavior, and Emotions

Intellect, or intelligence, refers to our ability to learn, understand, and act in a purposeful manner. The development of these abilities is influenced by heredity, learning experiences, and motivation. Intellect also includes memory, insight, judgment, orientation, attention span, concentration, problem solving, reasoning/logical thought, abstractions, and ambition. After a stroke, learning may be slower and incomplete because patients are less able to understand. The effects of stroke on the ability to think depend on the area of the brain affected.

Behavior is a complex process of actions and responses influenced by our thinking, emotions, and past experiences. Behavior also includes initiative, self-image, decision making, goal-directed behavior, and sexuality. Like other elements of cognition, it's a complex process that can be affected in any number of ways when damage to the brain occurs. For example, a person with brain damage may lose the ability to behave in ways we consider "normal." The result might be a show of anger, agitation, inappropriate laughter or crying, altered sex drive, or sleeping and eating disorders. When serious damage occurs to the frontal lobes of the brain, a patient may show a lack of motivation or may sit for hours unless prompted to act.

Damage to the parts of the brain that control emotions can result in personality changes. If the ability to control emotions is lost, patients may display emotionally extreme behaviors. They may cry over situations that would make other people happy. Other times, they may laugh inappropriately—at a funeral, for example. Such poor emotional control is known as emotional lability. It can be confusing to the patient and to observers since the patient's feelings will not be matched by his behaviors. To clarify the real emotion experienced by the patient, caregivers should simply ask the patient to describe what he is feeling, and compare this with the demonstrated behavior. Families might try changing the topic or distracting the patient to deter the inappropriate behavior.

Anger often accompanies personality changes. Patients who previously had loving and gentle manners may now seem very angry. This may be due in part to the overwhelming frustration of handling all the changes caused by the stroke. On the other hand, injury for some patients may have the opposite effect. They instead may become agreeable and cheerful. Often, these personality changes seem impulsive or even bizarre.

Depression

Of all the emotional changes that stroke patients may experience, depression is one that certainly deserves special mention. Understandably, the effects of a stroke can spark major depression. Imagine that you have spent weeks or months in a hospital, unable to function as you normally would. As the mental fog lifts, you realize that no matter how hard you try to imitate a therapist's movements, your arm and leg just won't move. The chance of ever walking around the house seems an improbability. Negotiating steps into your home is impossible. Everything you do from the time you wake until you go to sleep requires someone else's help. Your mind becomes

> **FAST FACT**
>
> According to the *Journal of Psychiatry and Neuroscience,* pathological laughing and crying (PLC) is a common emotional disorder following stroke. About 80 percent of those with PLC experience only pathological crying.

preoccupied with thoughts of never going home. This is an example of how depression can set in after a stroke.

In the early stages of injury to the brain, some people aren't really aware that they are unable to perform basic daily tasks. Their moods may be pleasant. Others may deny problems and deficits during much of their rehabilitation as inpatients. This may be a natural defense against the stress of such a major health problem. However, later on, depression may ensue as patients begin to grieve the loss of functions such as speech and walking.

Depression focuses energy and attention on the problem rather than on recovery. Patients may "shut down" and not participate in therapies. If the depression is severe enough, their physical performance may continue to decline over time.

Some studies conservatively estimate that about 8 percent of new stroke patients suffer minor depression, while

One of the impairments resulting from a stroke is diplopia, or double vision. **(AP Images/ Jonathan Fredin)**

up to 15 percent experience major depression. Other studies indicate an overall 40 percent rate of depression. Although research is not definitive, it seems that damage to the left side of the brain more frequently results in depression than damage to the right side.

Depression is a deep sadness, along with feelings of hopelessness and helplessness. . . .

Even medical professionals sometimes have difficulty identifying depression because the symptoms may be masked by a patient's dulled levels of consciousness, fatigue from therapy, altered sleeping and eating abilities, and the inability to communicate. People close to a patient who acts depressed should contact a physician immediately, especially if the patient expresses suicidal thoughts.

New Treatment Helps Restore Sight to Stroke Patients with Visual Damage

Kate Lunau

Kate Lunau is an assistant editor for *Maclean's* magazine. In the following viewpoint Lunau describes a newly developed technique that uses computer technology to help restore vision to stroke patients who have partial blindness. She says that a stroke patient's eyes may be functioning normally, but if there is damage to the visual processing centers of the brain, the patient will have vision loss. According to Lunau, researchers have developed a way to retrain the visual systems of such patients by having them practice a simple visual task on a computer screen—a technique inspired by physiotherapy used to improve motor skills in stroke patients. Lunau also cites another study in which video games that require hand-eye coordination were shown to improve vision in adults, which she says further demonstrates the validity of this technique.

SOURCE: Kate Lunau, "A Vision to Behold: New Computer-Based Exercises Help Retrain the Brain to See," *Maclean's,* May 25, 2009, p. 44. Copyright © 2009 by Rogers Communications. All rights reserved. Reproduced by permission.

Recovering from back surgery in a hospital bed, Millie Sauer, a self-confessed bookworm, pulled out a novel and began to read. She knew immediately that something was wrong. "Part of the page was grey. That had never happened before," says Sauer, 69. The hospital did some tests, she says, "and discovered I'd had a stroke."

Sauer struggled to cope with her partial loss of vision—one the doctors said was permanent. "I'd walk into the wall because I couldn't see on the left side," recalls Sauer, a retiree in Bismarck, N.D. Increasingly frustrated, she went online and found Krystel Huxlin, an associate professor at the University of Rochester [U of R] Eye Institute. "When I got a hold of Krystel, things started looking up," Sauer says.

Huxlin and her team recently made a stunning announcement: by doing a set of visual exercises on a computer, stroke patients suffering from partial blindness were able to regain some sight, offering hope for a condition that was once considered permanent. Indeed, computers are being used in novel ways to improve eyesight: in another study, video games were shown to actually boost vision in adults. Just as physical training can make a body stronger, visual training holds the potential to make us see better.

Recruiting Healthy Brain Regions

About one-quarter of stroke patients experience some vision loss, says Dr. Michael Hill, an associate professor at the University of Calgary's Hotchkiss Brain Institute and spokesperson for the Heart and Stroke Foundation of Canada. "After all, you don't see with your eyes," he explains. "You see with your brain." Information passes through the eyes to the primary visual cortex, the gateway through which it's fed to other parts of the brain and then processed into an image. "If damage [from a stroke] occurs along a visual pathway, you can lose vision," he says.

A stroke victim's eyes, though, are often perfectly fine—and continue to receive information, even if the brain doesn't know what to do with it. Huxlin's goal was to recruit healthy regions of the brain to bring that visual information into consciousness.

In the study, Huxlin's team recruited seven stroke victims, including Sauer, all of whom had suffered damage to the primary visual cortex. They were asked to stare at a small black square in the middle of a computer screen. Every few seconds, roughly 100 dots would appear within the patient's damaged visual field—meaning they were initially invisible. Moving in a cluster across the screen, the dots would twinkle into sight, then disappear. The patient had to indicate if the dots moved left or right, with a chime indicating the correct answer, giving the brain positive feedback. Participants did these exercises once or

A man uses the Nintendo Wii Sports boxing game to help him recover from a stroke. Scientists have discovered that video games that call for eye-hand coordination can help stroke patients who suffered partial blindness regain some lost eyesight. **(Adam Hart-Davis/Photo Researchers, Inc.)**

twice a day for up to 18 months, spending as much as 30 minutes at a time.

This type of visual training, Huxlin says, was inspired by physiotherapy that improves patients' motor skills after a stroke. "There's nothing wrong with the visual system; we just didn't know how to retrain it properly," she says. "Now, we do."

Using Video Games to Improve Vision

Huxlin isn't the only researcher employing computers to improve patients' eyesight. A separate study, also from the University of Rochester, showed video games can improve an adult's vision. In the study, led by Daphne Bavelier, 35 students were asked to play 50 hours of video games over nine weeks one summer. One group played first-person-shooter games Call of Duty 2 and Unreal Tournament 2004; the other played The Sims 2, a richly visual game that doesn't require the hand-eye coordination of the other two. By the end of the nine weeks, those who played shooter games showed a 43 per cent improvement in ability to discern close shades of grey (also known as contrast sensitivity, the main determinant of how well we see). The Sims players showed none.

Renjie Li is a U of R graduate student and co-author of the study. "Usually, laser eye surgery or eyeglasses are used to improve contrast sensitivity by changing the parameters of the eyeballs," he says. "Video games don't change your eyeballs, but they can change how your brain processes visual information." Action video games like Call of Duty 2 feature unpredictable events; they're fast-paced and require aiming skill, he explains. What's more, motivation and reward are built in. By devoting hours at a time to playing games, Li explains, subjects' brains learned how to process information more efficiently. Positive effects seemed to last up to a year.

FAST FACT

A small study reported in *Clinical Advisor* in 2009 found that three simple eye-movement tests diagnosed stroke more accurately than a magnetic resonance imaging scan.

Of course, computers aren't uniformly good for our eyes—sitting in front of a screen all day can lead to eye strain. "But what we're dealing with here is a bad brain, not bad eyes," Huxlin says. "This is the only way we know to retrain the brain to see." Huxlin hopes her treatment will become as widely available as physical rehab is today. "A lot of people just accept that there's nothing that can be done [for stroke-induced blindness]," she says. "They shouldn't have to."

Those who participated in Huxlin's study, Sauer included, managed to actually regain some of their lost eyesight. For Sauer, it made all the difference; she can even drive today, although she sticks to secondary roads, and still does the training every day. "I do have improvement in my vision; I can see it," she says. "As long as it keeps getting better, I will keep doing it."

Advanced Brain Mapping Research Will Improve Stroke Treatment

Emily Singer

Emily Singer is the senior biomedicine editor at *Technology Review*, an independent media company owned by the Massachusetts Institute of Technology. In the following viewpoint Singer reports on research that is being done into how networks of communication between different brain regions are disrupted in stroke patients. She refers to one study that found that patients who had motor or visual problems in only one side of their body also showed disrupted communication between the two hemispheres of their brain. The more the patients were impaired, the greater the level of disruption in hemisphere communication. According to the author, better understanding of how brain communication networks are disrupted by stroke damage will enable researchers to more accurately target specific treatments to particular patients. For example, similar motor impairments in two different patients could be caused by different network disruptions, and thus require different treatments to heal the damage.

SOURCE: Emily Singer, "Brain Maps for Stroke Treatment," *Technology Review,* March 29, 2010. technologyreview.com. Copyright © 2010 by Technology Review, Inc. All rights reserved. Reproduced by permission.

After a stroke, the brain suffers more broadly than just at the spot that was starved of blood. New research, which uses brain imaging to examine connections between different parts of the brain, shows that communication between the left and right hemispheres is often disrupted; the greater the disruption, the more profound the patient's impairment in movement or vision. Researchers hope to use the approach to predict which patients are mostly likely to recover on their own and which will need the most intensive therapy.

The study is part of a broader effort to incorporate the brain mapping technology into post-stroke assessment, including new clinical trials testing experimental drugs and physical therapy in combination with imaging. Mapping brain connectivity and recovery may give scientists a better measure of which treatments most effectively enhance the brain's innate plasticity—its ability to rewire—and when the brain is best primed for repair.

"The kind of information we're getting from neural imaging studies is giving us a better understanding of the kind of changes that are important during recovery," says Alexandre Carter, a neurologist at Washington University, in St. Louis, who led the study.

Localized Dysfunction Disrupts Larger Brain Networks

Stroke patients typically undergo an MRI [magnetic resonance imaging] to identify the precise location of their stroke. But these brain scans don't show how the damaged part of the brain fits into the larger network—the neural connections that feed into and out of this spot. Just as a delay at one station of a subway system can affect service at numerous stops and subway lines, dysfunction in a localized part of the brain disrupts activity in several different parts.

In the new study, researchers assessed this disruption by creating a functional connectivity map of the brain in

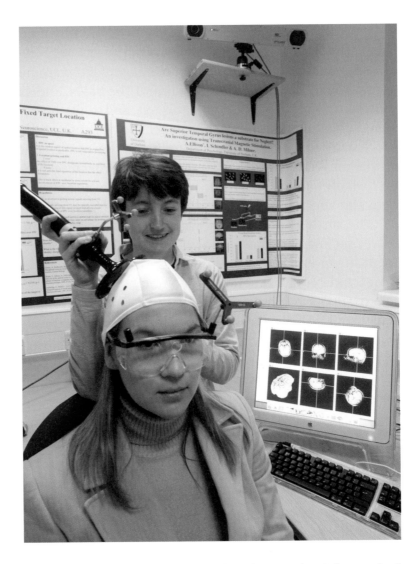

A woman undergoes image-guided transcranial magnetic stimulation brain mapping. The area targeted is mapped to a scan of her brain shown on a computer behind her. (© Simon Fraser/University of Durham/Photo Researchers, Inc.)

people who had recently suffered a stroke. They asked patients to lie quietly in an MRI machine and used functional MRI [fMRI], an indirect measure of neural activity, to detect spontaneous fluctuations in brain activity. Brain areas that are well-connected will fluctuate in synchrony [simultaneously], providing an indirect way of mapping the brain's networks.

As is often the case with stroke, they found that patients' visual or motor problems were limited to just one side of the body, such as a weak left hand or an inability to pay attention to objects in the left side of the field of vision. (Because the left side of the brain typically controls the right side of the body and vice versa, a stroke on one side of the brain will affect the opposite side of the body.) But the researchers found that patients with these symptoms had disruptions in the connections between the two hemispheres. And the level of disruption between the two halves of the brain correlated to the severity of their impairment. "The physical damage has repercussions all throughout the network, like a ripple effect, even in areas that aren't physically damaged," says Carter.

Analyzing Network Dysfunction to Improve Treatment

The research, published this month [March 2010] in *Annals of Neurology*, is the first step in a multiyear project assessing how to predict how well people will recover from stroke. Researchers will repeat the brain scanning and behavioral testing months after the patients' strokes to see how both change over time.

Carter and others ultimately aim to use the technology to better target stroke treatments. "It's important to know what lies behind recovery, because we want to have a brain-based understanding of new treatments," says James Rowe, a neuroscientist at Cambridge University, in the U.K., who was not involved in the study. In addition, he says, because this kind of scan can be done very early, "we might be able to classify patients who would benefit from one type of therapy or another."

Two patients who have similar motor impairments might actually have very different disruptions to their brain networks and therefore benefit from different types of treatment. For example, not everyone responds to constraint-induced movement therapy, in which the

FAST FACT

New Scientist reported in 2011 that Israeli scientists had successfully created an artificial rat cerebellum (a brain structure regulating movement), demonstrating that artificial brain structures might someday restore function to stroke patients.

Constraint-Induced Therapy (CIT)

Contstraint-induced therapy (CIT) is a type of rehabilitation therapy that relies on neural plasticity, the capacity of the brain to rewire itself to heal damage. A stroke patient's unaffected limb is constrained for periods of time to encourage increased use of a limb affected by stroke while performing various tasks.

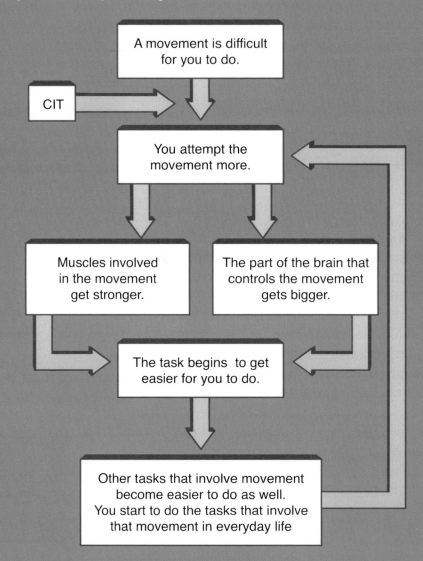

A movement is difficult for you to do.

CIT

You attempt the movement more.

Muscles involved in the movement get stronger.

The part of the brain that controls the movement gets bigger.

The task begins to get easier for you to do.

Other tasks that involve movement become easier to do as well. You start to do the tasks that involve that movement in everyday life

Taken from: Peter G. Levine. *Stronger After Stroke: Your Roadmap to Recovery*. New York: Demos Health, 2009, p.72.

strong arm is bound, forcing the patient to use their weak arm. Analysis of network dysfunction might help predict which patients will benefit from this treatment.

The research is part of a broader effort to capitalize on the inherent neural plasticity that is present even in the adult brain. "There is more and more interest in changes in the brain that occur at more chronic stages of stroke," says Rick Dijkhuizen, a neurobiologist at University Medical Center Utrecht, in the Netherlands, who was not involved in the current work. "Increasing evidence suggests that the brain is able to reorganize even in patients [whose strokes occurred a long time ago], and this gives us opportunities to look at stroke therapies to promote this organization."

CHAPTER 2

Controversies Surrounding Stroke

Stem Cell Therapy to Treat Stroke Shows Promise

Aaron Saenz

Aaron Saenz graduated from Harvard University, where he studied physics, and earned a master's degree from Rice University in atomic molecular and optical physics. In the following viewpoint Saenz argues that stem cells have great potential to treat brain damage caused by stroke. He describes research being done at the University of Glasgow in Scotland, in which fetal stem cells were injected into the brain of a stroke survivor. According to Saenz, studies using animals have demonstrated that such an injection can heal scar tissue, reduce inflammation, and stimulate the growth of new blood vessels. Although the author stresses the preliminary nature of this research, he says that it is reasonable to expect some degree of healing and recovery of lost functions.

Photo on facing page. A researcher pipettes stem cells from a culturing tube. The use of some types of stem cells in medical research has caused controversy. (© Pasquale Sorrentino/Photo Researchers, Inc.)

SOURCE: Aaron Saenz, "Scotland Injects Stem Cells into Man's Brain to Heal Stroke Damage," *Singularity Hub,* November 22, 2010. singularityhub.com. Copyright © 2010 by Singularity Hub. All rights reserved. Reproduced by permission.

T here are few medical calamities that terrify as many people as a stroke. Of those that survive the sudden blocks or ruptures in their brain, nearly half suffer permanent damage that will never be repaired. Researchers in Scotland could be changing that. The University of Glasgow's Institute of Neuroscience and Psychology recently injected fetal stem cells into the brain of a stroke survivor 18 months after his near fatal injury. The man, who is in his 60s, is the first patient in a clinical trial to test the safety and feasibility of using stem cells to repair ischaemic stroke damage (which accounts for 80% of all strokes). According to the University of Glasgow, his injection is pioneering the use of stem cells for this condition, and the purveyor of these cells, ReNeuron, says it is the first UK [United Kingdom] company to get approval for a human stem cell clinical trial in the country. While it will be months before we are likely to know if the treatment has helped heal the damage in this man's brain, the possibility of success is yet another sign that stem cells are the most promising technology of the early 21st Century.

Look through the hospital beds in the UK [United Kingdom] and you'll find that nearly one in four of the people in long-term care are there because they suffered a stroke. There are 150,000 stroke victims in the UK and 700,000 in the US each year. Because strokes often leave patients alive but critically impaired they are responsible for billions in healthcare costs. That price tag is only going to increase as the global population continues to age. Finding the right therapy will be critically important in the years ahead.

FAST FACT

A study published in the journal *Stem Cells* in 2012 showed recovery of up to 83 percent of sensorimotor function in rats with stroke damage in the striatial brain region after an injection of ReNeuron's CTX stem cells.

Promising Results from Animal Testing

Stem cells, then, provide a unique opportunity to improve the lives of millions while saving billions, which is the reason this Pilot Investigation of Stem Cells in Stroke (PISCES) was begun. ReNeuron's therapy, ReN001, is derived from the cells of a 12 week old fetus collected in the US (the cells are sometimes designated as CTX). At that phase of development the cells are already differentiating into nerve lineages. It's hoped that the stem cells, injected into the putamen [a deep brain structure], will release chemicals that stimulate the growth of new neurons and blood vessels. Animal models have already shown how similar injections can reduce inflammation and heal scar tissue associated with ischaemic stroke, as well as promote the growth of new vascular tissue.

There is a lot riding on this first unnamed male patient. While the University of Glasgow and ReNeuron plan on having 11 more clinical trial participants (all between 60 and 85, and all 6 to 24 months after stroke), they have yet to be completely approved. Safety monitoring agencies in the UK will need to review the first patient's condition in December [2010], and only after that will the others be enrolled and given injections. Varying amounts of CTX will be used. The first patient received around 2 million

A scientist and a lab technician examine the stem cells centrifuged from blood. Animal studies regarding stem cell therapy for stroke patients has been promising.
(© AP Images/Rob Bratney-Missourian)

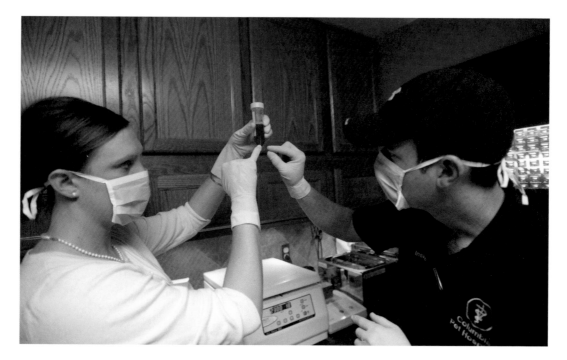

Why Embryonic Stem Cells Are Special

Embryonic stem cells are *undifferentiated*, which means they have the potential to turn into any other kind of cell. They can become blood cells, muscle cells, or neural cells.

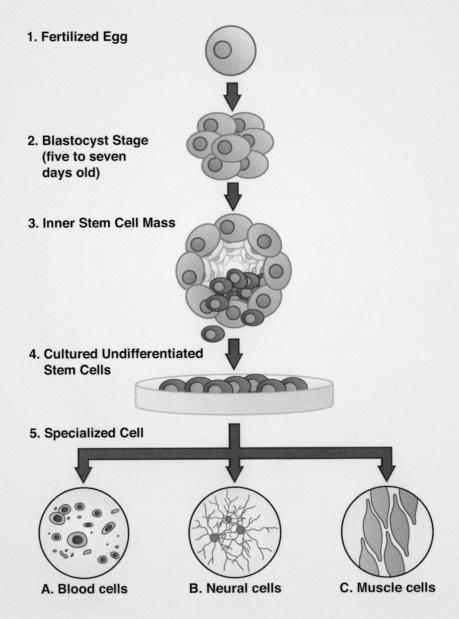

1. Fertilized Egg

2. Blastocyst Stage (five to seven days old)

3. Inner Stem Cell Mass

4. Cultured Undifferentiated Stem Cells

5. Specialized Cell

A. Blood cells

B. Neural cells

C. Muscle cells

Taken from: http://stemcells-research.net.

cells, while subsequent injections in other subjects will increase to 5M, 10M, and 20M. Patients will be monitored for 2 years after injection, with follow up examinations continuing into the long term. Because the fetal stem cells are already differentiated into nerve lineages their risk for producing tumors and cancer is deemed to be less.

Great Potential for Healing

This study (which has a registered clinical trial number in the US) is really only aimed at determining safety and feasibility. As such, doctors in Glasgow and representatives at ReNeuron aren't overselling the fetal stem cell therapy at this point. Still, there's a reasonable expectation that patients could heal some level of brain damage, and possibly regain some lost motor skills and functions. The real dream would be for stem cell therapies to completely reverse the changes caused by the stroke. That level of healing is far from expected in this clinical trial, if it is even possible at all.

Like other fetal and embryonic stem cell projects, ReN001 has the potential to heal many people using the same line of cells. The stem cell injections are almost like drug doses. Unlike many other projects that use the patient's own stem cells (autologous transplants), here ReNeuron provides the cells for each patient. We've seen similar work in the US with Geron's spinal cord injury trials, but in general US stem cell research (outside of California) seems to be lagging behind in this field. China, meanwhile, has been going on a trial and error rampage for the last few years, injecting stem cells into every part of the body. Chances are that they've treated a stroke victim at some point with some kind of stem cells, but without the rigorous methodology of this UK study. Hopefully PISCES, which has such an enormous potential to heal patients, will not only lead to success in these UK trials, but encourage similar work to accelerate in the rest of the world. There are a lot of grandchildren out there who'd like to be able to play with their grandparents. Strokes can rob us of those experiences, but stem cells could bring them back.

Stem Cell Therapy for Stroke and Other Acquired Brain Injuries Is Risky and Unproven

David H. Gorski

David H. Gorski is a surgical oncologist at the Barbara Ann Karmanos Cancer Institute and a member of the faculty of the Graduate Program in Cancer Biology at Wayne State University in Detroit, Michigan. In the following viewpoint Gorski argues that disreputable clinics are currently offering stem cell treatments to cure brain damage from strokes, with no scientific support for their claims that these treatments are safe or effective. He gives the example of a Canadian woman named Alda Byers, who suffered a brain stem stroke, following which her family took her to a Mexican stem cell clinic for treatment. According to the author, when he looked at the website for the clinic, he found no reliable scientific evidence to back up its claims, but he did find signs of quackery—such as claims that the clinic's treatment cures many different conditions. Gorski suggests that such stem cell clinics are selling unproven treatments to people for financial gain.

SOURCE: David H. Gorski, "Stem Cell Therapy for 'Locked-In' Syndrome?," *Respectful Insolence,* April 5, 2010. scienceblogs.com. Copyright © 2010 by David H Gorski. All rights reserved. Reproduced by permission.

The concept of being "locked in" [totally paralyzed but able to hear, see, and feel] both fascinates and horrifies me. I have a hard time imagining a worse fate, and stories of the locked-in hold a special fascination for me.

That's why I was disturbed to find out about a woman in Toronto [Ontario, Canada] named Alda Byers who is . . . locked in. . . . The case of Alda Byers involves what is likely (but not certainly) quackery coupled with a number of thorny ethical issues that are hinted at, but barely touched upon, in a story by Michele Mandel entitled ["]Trapped in her own body, docs won't help: Woman denied stem cell treatment that offered hope.["] The title alone was painful to read because it paints the doctors who won't help Byers pursue stem cell woo [quackery] being heartless and blocking her from her last chance at a cure from her horrific state.

Stem Cell Treatment for Brain Stem Stroke

The story begins:

> Freedom flickered so elusively close, with a joyous new wiggle of her toes, with the thrilling turning of her head.
>
> For Alda Byers, imprisoned by a rare, paralyzing brain stem stroke, a controversial stem-cell treatment in Mexico last fall [2009] seemed to deliver on its promise of improvement.
>
> But now all her progress has come to an abrupt end and her family believes it's Canadian medical reticence that is standing in her way.
>
> The pretty 52-year-old remains trapped in her hospital bed at West Park, her world confined by walls brightly decorated with loving cards and dozens upon dozens of photos of her family, friends and beloved dog.

Yes, the article itself, in the name of "human interest," has let us know that the Canadian medical establishment

A cell therapy lab processes stem cells. Stem cell opponents say disreputable clinics are offering stem cell treatments to cure brain damage from stroke with no scientific support for their claims.
(© Véronique Burger/ Photo Researchers, Inc.)

is apparently too uncaring to help the Byers family achieve its ends and save the unfortunate Mrs. Byers from her fate. The article even continues with a real, live, honest-to-goodness testimonial:

> With the help of hundreds of friends, they held two fund-raisers and put together the thousands of dollars they need to get her a stem-cell transplant last September in Cancun.
>
> As first, the results were astounding.
>
> She could suddenly move her neck from side to side. She could open her mouth and form an "O."
>
> She could wiggle her toes and fingers. She could laugh and even breathe on her own for short spells. For someone who couldn't move at all, it was a breathtaking promise of what lay ahead.

Soon after arriving [home] back at West Park, with Byers happily demonstrating her new tricks for all her visitors, they received a follow-up e-mail from her Mexican doctor: to continue the stem cells' work, she'd need to take a cocktail of drugs for the next six-to-eight weeks.

They never anticipated any problem with a Toronto doctor writing the prescription. The three drugs— erythropoeitin, filgastrim and somatotropin—are not rare or experimental. The first two are generally used for anemia, renal failure and chemotherapy, the third has been used in children and athletes as a growth hormone.

Hallmarks of Quackery

Even though these are drugs that are approved and available and even though doctors can prescribe drugs off label, apparently the family has had difficulty finding a doctor willing to prescribe the drugs requested. This is not surprising, given that these are powerful drugs with serious potential side effects, particularly the first two. Indeed, one wonders why the clinic in Mexico peddling this stem cell woo would consider erythropoietin, which stimulates red blood cell production, and filgastrim, which stimulates white blood cell production, to be essential to its protocol. These are not generally substances that would stimulate the growth of new neurons from stem cells. . . . In the absence of evidence demonstrating the efficacy of whatever "stem cell" protocol the Mexican clinic had prescribed and absent a demonstration that this protocol required these drugs, the Canadian physicians approached to prescribe them were right to be wary and reluctant.

When I first saw this story, I did a little Googling to learn about Byers' story. I found out that the specific clinic to which her family took her last summer was that of Calvin Cao from Stem Cell Therapy International Inc. [SCTI], in Tijuana. It's a highly dubious-appearing clinic whose website contains several [of] the hallmarks of quackery, specifically claims of efficacy for many, many conditions, including diabetes, cirrhosis, and neurological conditions, among the more common diseases. Amazingly, SCTI also claims efficacy of its particular stem cell woo for adhesions of the abdominal cavity after surgery and the "rejuvination" (spelling error copied from the website) of women after menopause, both applications I haven't heard before for stem cells. The latter of these is described using word salad devoid of any real science behind it:

> We developed the regimen of biological preparation introductions, its characteristics and necessary dosage. As opposed to the treatment of androgenous disorders, in this case we used 10–12 week preparations with XX genotypes. Before carrying out treatment with preparations, a profound study of somatic and gynecologic anamnesis in view of contra-indications to hormonal therapy, mammography and bio-chemical examination, ultrasound of organs of the small pelvis on the 5–7th days of the menstrual cycle are made.

From what I can figure out, SCTI seems to be using some sort of cell-based bioidentical hormone therapy, but it's hard to tell from the word salad science on its website. Regardless, apparently its woo is not limited merely to stem cell woo.

No Peer-Reviewed Evidence

Not surprisingly, I could not find on its website a single instance of peer-reviewed research directly supporting the efficacy of the "biological preparations" administered by SCTI. The website cites thousands of articles apparently culled from PubMed searches on certain keywords, but it doesn't provide, as far as I can find, a single example of a well-designed clinical trial published in a peer-reviewed journal demonstrating that their methodology has a measurable therapeutic effect on the conditions for which SCTI claims efficacy for its methods. They make the excuse that the real reports that allegedly show the efficacy for their methods are all in Russian and German and not indexed in MEDLINE [US National Library of Medicine's database of biomedical and life sciences literature]. . . .

Also nowhere on the SCTI website could I find evidence that any of its preparations actually contain real human stem cells, pluripotent cells that can be induced to differentiate into many, if not any, organ. In fact, I'd be highly suspicious of their preparations and that they can even make stem cells suitable for attempts at stem cell therapy. The website lists a lot of "applications" for their stem cells, but don't include a link to a single scientific paper supporting these claims. There is no detailed outcome data to show that they have results better than what could be expected using the standard of care, much less high quality data from randomized clinical trials demonstrating efficacy of their stem cell preparations. In brief, SCTI shows all the hallmarks of peddling pseudoscience to the Byers, all for $50,000 for six daily injections of "stem cells," a sum that ballooned to $150,000 when all other expenses, including a private plane for transportation, were added in.

> **FAST FACT**
>
> According to a 2009 article in *Nursing,* many cases of locked-in syndrome go undetected, as it tends to be misdiagnosed as coma, minimally conscious state, or persistent vegetative state.

No Objective Evidence of Improvement

Regardless of one's opinion of the SCTI clinic (and I have made my opinion of the extreme dubiousness of any of its claims known), the question remains of what to do with Mrs. Byers now that she has returned and her husband is claiming significant improvement. First, we must remember that there appears to be no objective evidence of concrete improvement other than the word of Byers and her husband. We have no detailed neurological examinations documented before and after the treatment, for example. While it is possible that the improvement claimed is real and due to the "stem cell therapy," it is also unlikely. We have no idea whether some of these movements were possible before the treatment and the perceived improvement the result of expectation effect and confirmation bias or whether there was a real improvement. Again, there is no reported objective documentation of these improvements, and there needs to be. I can understand Mr. Byers' frustration here.

> "It's like hitting your head against the wall," says Byers, 60, waving a thick file of e-mails from physicians turning them down.
>
> "Everybody wants case studies," he complains. "But somebody with a brain stem stroke is one in a million and how many of them have undergone stem cell treatment? None."

On the other hand, this is a bit of a straw man. I'd bet that most of those doctors who want case studies would understand that locked-in syndrome is (mercifully) rare and would be willing to accept evidence from case studies of stroke victims who suffered less devastating neurological damage than locked-in syndrome or victims of spinal cord injury. For example, if a stroke victim with a complete hemiparesis [weakness] of one side of their body were to demonstrate documentable, objective improvement in the affected side after the stem cell therapy, that would be a legitimate case study that might convince me there was something going on worthy of further study. If a patient with a complete transection of his spinal cord and complete paralysis below the waist for three years suddenly could move his feet after stem cell therapy by SCTI, that would be suggestive evidence that might convince me that it's worth continuing with the SCTI stem cell therapy in Mrs. Byers' case, given that her current condition is so horrific and there is currently nothing medicine can do to ameliorate or reverse it. I can find no such case studies with any objective documentation of improvement in neurological function beyond what could be expected in the natural course of their condition in patients with severe neurological injury like stroke or spinal cord transection.

Ethical Considerations

In the case of Mrs. Byers, there are at least two major ethical considerations at play, along with the problem of pitting science-based medicine versus stem cell hucksters selling what is likely to be false hope. First, there is the ethical precept of "First, do no harm." Prescribing drugs like erythropoietin has a real risk of doing harm. Also impacting the case is the ethical precept against performing experimentation on humans without sound science and extensive preclinical data to prove a reasonable degree of plausibility. In this, the stem cell therapy offered by SCTI

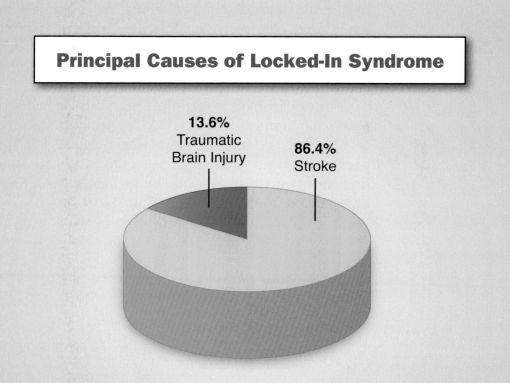

Principal Causes of Locked-In Syndrome

13.6%
Traumatic
Brain Injury

86.4%
Stroke

Taken from: J. León-Carrión et al. "The Locked-In Syndrome: A Syndrome Looking for a Therapy." *Brain Injury,* vol. 16, no. 7, July 2002, pp. 571–582.

fails utterly, given how little evidence appears to support it. Even worse, SCTI charges $50,000 per round of treatments for what is at best a highly experimental treatment not ready for prime time and at worst pure quackery. Without strong evidence for the efficacy of such a treatment, it is in general unethical to charge so much money for it, and it pains me to see these stem cell clinics taking advantage of patients as sad and desperate as Alva Byers.

I could understand it if a physician, hearing Mr. Byers' plea, decided that Alva's condition was so terrible that he might as well grant their wishes and prescribe the drugs SCTI requested. I might disagree, but I could understand someone who says, in essence, that Mrs. Byers' current condition is a fate worse than death and, even if there really hasn't been any evidence of objective improvement due to the alleged stem cell therapy, there's nothing to lose by giving her the three drug cocktail that's supposed to keep the stem cell treatment going. What I can neither understand nor forgive are companies like SCTI peddling unproven and likely ineffective varieties of "stem cell" therapy to desperate patients like Mrs. Byers, all in order to separate them from their money.

Nor can I forgive reporting as irresponsible and supportive of companies like SCTI victimizing patients like Mrs. Byers as demonstrated by Michele Mandel. Such reporting serves no purpose other than to encourage other desperate patients to seek out companies like SCTI and be separated from their money as well.

The Rapidly Rising Rate of Stroke in the Young Needs to Be Taken Seriously

David Katz

David Katz is the founding director of Yale University's Prevention Research Center at Griffin Hospital, founder of the Integrative Medicine Center at Griffin Hospital, and author of *Nutrition in Clinical Practice: A Comprehensive, Evidence-Based Manual for the Practitioner*. In the following viewpoint Katz says that stroke is becoming increasingly common in children, especially in those aged five to fourteen. He claims that the increased stroke risk in the young is a predictable outcome of such trends as an increase in obesity, hypertension and diabetes in that age group, factors which are known to increase the likelihood of stroke. According to the author, type 2 diabetes, which used to be called adult onset diabetes, is increasingly found in children less than ten years old. Katz argues that policies and practices that encourage healthy eating and exercise should be adopted so that the trend of increased stroke and other cardiovascular health problems in the young can be reversed.

SOURCE: David Katz, "Why the Rising Rate of Youth Strokes Was Predictable," *Huffington Post*, February 2, 2011. huffingtonpost.com. Copyright © 2011 by David Katz. All rights reserved. Reproduced by permission.

The American Stroke Association's International Stroke Conference 2011 was held last week [January 2011] in Los Angeles. Among the many important research findings reported was this bit of profoundly disquieting news: strokes are occurring with increasing frequency in people under age 35. Worse still, a marked increase in the rate of stroke was noted in children ages five to 14.

As a physician who has seen far too much bad stuff happen to far too many good people over the years, I truly can't imagine much worse than a stroke in a child. Formally a "cerebrovascular accident," induced more often by ischemia and less often by intracranial bleeding, a stroke is to the brain what a myocardial infarction (heart attack) is to the heart: part of the organ dies. A child has a stroke and part of a brain that should be thriving, burgeoning with newly acquired experience and knowledge dies. And with it dies some function, perhaps the ability to speak, or the ability to move one side of the body. With it dies childhood.

That this is a trend in modern epidemiology is both tragedy and travesty. The researchers readily acknowledge they don't know for sure why stroke rates, declining in adults over age 50, are rising in children and young adults. The study in question, by investigators at the CDC [Centers for Disease Control and Prevention], was simply a review of hospitalization records between 1994 and 2007. The analysis was designed to show what, but not why.

But that does not preclude some educated guesses, by the researchers themselves and the rest of us. The decline in strokes in older adults is almost certainly due to better treatment of hypertension, the leading cause of stroke, and to a lesser extent the modification of other risk factors for cardiovascular disease, such as lipid-lowering with statin drugs. Such vulnerabilities are routinely being sought, found and modified in adults known to be in the at-risk group.

Obesity, Diabetes, and Hypertension

But of course, stroke and ischemic heart disease are not expected in the pediatric age group. Historically, there has been no cause to look systematically for risk factors of vascular disease in this population, let alone apply the use of antihypertensives and statin drugs to avert calamity.

It is nothing short of calamity that it has come to this. The researchers' best guess, and mine, is that the migration of stroke down the age curve is being propelled by epidemic obesity, diabetes and rising rates of hypertension in our children. We can choose to be shocked by the advent of stroke in children, but it was, in fact, predictable.

Predictions need not be about what comes true. Grim predictions can motivate preventive responses so the adversities they foretell never materialize. Forewarned can be forearmed.

I have, for years, been predicting heart disease as a routine, pediatric condition—in the hopes it would never come true.

The logic behind my rather lonely rants on this topic has been quite straightforward. A group of experts in cardiovascular medicine called the Adult Treatment Panel of The National Cholesterol Education Program issues guidelines for health care providers in the identification and management of cardiac risk factors in our patients. Those guidelines tell us that we should treat our patients with diabetes as if they already were known to have coronary heart disease, because the link between the two is so strong.

> **FAST FACT**
>
> A child who has had a stroke has a 13 percent chance of having a second stroke, according to a 2010 article in *Family Practice News.*

"Adult Onset" Diabetes Is Now Seen in Children

When I went to medical school, I learned about two kinds of diabetes mellitus: juvenile onset and adult onset. What we now call type 2 diabetes is diagnosed more and more commonly in children under the age of 10. But less than

Stroke is becoming more common in children due to increases in childhood obesity, hypertension, and diabetes. (© Gusto/ Photo Researchers, Inc.)

a generation ago, this very condition was appropriately called "adult onset," because it occurred almost exclusively in overweight, middle-age adults.

If one chronic disease of midlife can migrate down the age curve to become a condition of childhood, what basis did we have to think that others wouldn't follow? What the Adult Treatment Panel says about diabetes in adults—that it can be assumed to signal the presence of heart disease—is true in children, too, until proved otherwise. We have little cause to think diabetes does different damage to small bodies than to larger ones.

So, when 16, 17 and 18 year-olds have had adult onset diabetes already for a decade or more, shouldn't we expect to start seeing them in emergency rooms with angina pectoris and myocardial infarction? I have long thought we should.

And regrettably, I have had incremental indications over time that my predictions were coming true. Several years ago, I made my usual grave prediction about the advent of coronary disease in teenagers in Atlanta, Georgia, at an American College of Cardiology meeting there. One of the physicians in my audience told me she had heard that some 7,000 teenagers had heart attacks in the U.S. the year prior. I could not confirm that statistic, but there is more and more medical literature referring to this trend.

I gave a talk in Missouri a few years back, after which a dietitian in the audience told me about a 17-year-old boy whose care she was involved in, who had undergone a triple coronary bypass. To the best of her knowledge, this boy had no unusual genetic predisposition to heart disease. Just obesity, type 2 diabetes at an early age, and the obvious, predictable consequences.

Exercise and Healthy Diet

When I first started making a fuss about this 10 years back or more, my audiences were dubious and uncertain of my reasoning. More recently, they have seemed less stunned, more convinced and deeply concerned. Now they are starting to provide evidence to prove me right. This is a very unhappy trend. And frankly, while I was warning against the advent of angina as an adolescent rite of passage alongside acne, even I didn't envision strokes in children under the age of 10.

Which brings us back to the new research findings. We don't know with certainty the causes of a rising rate of stroke in our children. But with the stakes this high, do we really want to wait for more data? The best way to predict the future is to create it, and I would very much like to predict a future in which the only stroke my children and grandchildren need worry about is the stroke of a dissatisfied teacher's red pen.

Strokes per 10,000 Hospitalizations, 1994–1995 and 2006–2007

Male
Female

Number of Hospitalizations

100
90
80
70
60
50
40
30
20
10
0

9.8%
14.8%
3.6%
4.2%
36.0%
52.9%
21.9%
30.0%

Ages 15–34, 1994–1995
Ages 15–34, 2006–2007
Ages 15–34, 1994–1995
Ages 15–34, 2006–2007
Ages 35–44, 1994–1995
Ages 35–44, 2006–2007
Ages 35–44, 1994–1995
Ages 35–44, 2006–2007

Stroke Victim by Age/Year

Taken from: "Strokes Surge Among Young." *H & HN Hospitals and Health Networks,* April 2011, p. 52.

Modern trends in chronic disease constitute a crisis. A crisis is a dangerous opportunity, because recognition of danger inspires will for change.

We can change our ways, and protect our children and grandchildren from the heart attacks and strokes of unkind fate—by becoming a society that honors feet and forks as master levers of medical destiny, rather than relying so heavily on stethoscopes, scalpels and statins in the aftermath of disaster. By doing all that is required to make eating well and being active lie along the path of least resistance.

The list of interventions to get us there is long, but not complicated. Every policy or practice that isn't a part of the solution is a part of the problem—and a potential threat to a child. Vote accordingly.

In defense of our children, we should act—even as we await data to verify likely causes. We should not attribute lamentable trends in epidemiology to unkind strokes of fate. The fate in question is almost certainly in our own hands. The bell curve of chronic disease is tolling ever more loudly for us all.

It is past time to answer the alarm with the urgency it warrants.

Chiropractic Adjustments Can Cause Strokes

Harriet Hall

Harriet Hall is a retired family physician and former US Air Force flight surgeon who writes about medicine, science, and critical thinking at her blog *The SkepDoc*. She is a contributing editor to *Skeptic* and *Skeptical Inquirer*. In the following viewpoint Hall claims that chiropractic adjustments to the neck pose a significant risk of stroke, although the exact magnitude of the risk is unknown. She says that according to one estimate, 20 percent of one type of stroke is caused by chiropractic adjustments, and she adds that many insurance payments for chiropractic malpractice are due to strokes. According to the author, chiropractors are aware of the stroke risk but often fail to adequately inform patients of the risk or ask permission before performing neck adjustments. Hall argues that patients have the right to be fully informed of the stroke risk involved in this type of chiropractic adjustment.

SOURCE: Harriet Hall, "Chiropractic and Stroke," *Science-Based Medicine,* April 29, 2008. sciencebasedmedicine.org. Copyright © 2008 by Harriet Hall. All rights reserved. Reproduced by permission.

I wonder how many people have heard that chiropractic neck adjustments can cause strokes. It isn't exactly common knowledge. One organization is trying to raise public awareness through signs on the side of city buses (Injured by a Chiropractor? Call this number) and through TV commercials. I had never heard about this phenomenon myself until a few years ago, when I heard it mentioned on an episode of Alan Alda's *Scientific American Frontiers.* I questioned his accuracy, but I quickly found confirmation in the medical literature.

A typical case was that of 24 year old Kristi Bedenbaugh who saw her chiropractor for sinus headaches. During a neck manipulation she suffered a brain stem stroke and she died three days later. Autopsy revealed that the manipulation had split the inside walls of both of her vertebral arteries, causing the walls to balloon and block the blood supply to the lower part of her brain. Additional studies concluded that blood clots had formed on the days the manipulation took place. The chiropractor later paid a $1000 fine.

The two vertebral arteries run straight up the back of the neck passing through holes in the sides of each neck vertebra. When the head turns, the "tethered" artery is drastically kinked.

Because of this kinking, it is particularly susceptible to injury. Even a simple thing like extending the neck back over the basin for hair washing at the beauty salon has been known to cause a stroke. The artery is elastic, but with hardening of the arteries, with cholesterol plaques, with trauma (like automobile accidents) or simply with rapid stretching, the delicate lining of the artery can tear. It is easy to imagine how a rapid, forceful thrust by a chiropractor could cause damage.

Delayed Stroke

Sometimes the damage is immediate and the patient collapses on the chiropractor's table. Sometimes mild symptoms start immediately and progress after the patient

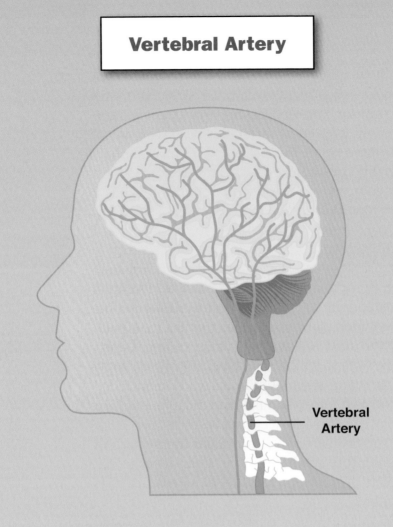

Vertebral Artery

Vertebral
Artery

Taken from: http://chiro.org/LINKS/GRAPHICS/VERTEBRAL_ARTERY.JPG.

leaves the chiropractor's office. Sometimes the tear is a
small one and it clots over; then days later the clot breaks
loose, travels to the brain and causes a delayed stroke. By
this time, the patient may not connect his sudden collapse to the previous visit to the chiropractor.

Chiropractors are well aware of the risk. They discuss
it in their journals and online forums. They have tried
to find ways to screen patients for high risk, but there
is no reliable way to do so. Strokes are a major reason
for chiropractic malpractice insurance payouts—9% of

claims paid by the major chiropractic insurer in 2002, the only year for which I was able to find statistics. Some chiropractors are now asking patients to sign an informed consent form before manipulations. If asked, most chiropractors downplay the risk, saying it occurs in less than one in a million manipulations. Many (perhaps most) chiropractors do not mention the risk at all.

Most alarming: some chiropractors perform these neck adjustments with no warning and without permission. I met a woman who still walks with a limp and has other residual impairments from a chiropractic stroke. She went to her chiropractor for a shoulder problem and thought he was going to massage her shoulder muscles. She did not want him to manipulate her neck, did not give him permission, and didn't realize what he was doing until he suddenly twisted her neck. She collapsed on the table and nearly died.

How often can a stroke be attributed to neck manipulation? We really don't know. Estimates have varied from one in ten million manipulations to one in 40,000. I should clarify that only one specific type of stroke, basilar stroke, has been linked to chiropractic. It has been estimated that about 20% of all basilar strokes are due to spinal manipulations. This would work out to about 1300 a year in the U.S. But we just don't know, because it has not been properly studied. Carotid artery strokes have also been reported after chiropractic treatments. Chiropractors do not follow up on every patient. Patients who have delayed strokes may never see their chiropractor again, so chiropractors would naturally tend to underestimate the risk. Many of these diagnoses are missed because the vertebral arteries are not typically examined on autopsy.

Benefit Versus Risk

One study of patients under the age of 45 who had this kind of stroke showed that they were 5 times more likely to have visited a chiropractor in the preceding week than control patients. In the past, neurologists treating stroke patients simply did not ask patients about chiropractic; and when they started asking, they started finding. There have been deaths. There have been court cases. In 2002, a group of Canadian neurologists issued a statement of concern to the public, recommending vigilance, education, informed consent, and other measures to protect the public. Awareness is rising, and injured patients have formed organizations in the US, Canada, and the UK both for support and for litigation.

FAST FACT

A 2001 British study found that none of thirty-five cases of neurological complications—including seven strokes—following chiropractic manipulation were reported in medical journals, suggesting such cases are highly under-reported.

Defensive chiropractors have tried to counteract the growing body of evidence with studies like this one [B.P. Symons et al., "Internal Forces Sustained by the Vertebral Artery During Spinal Manipulative Therapy," *Journal of Manipulative and Physiological Therapeutics*, October 25, 2002, pp. 504–510], which concluded that "SMT [Spinal Manipulation Therapy] resulted in strains to the VA [Vertebral Artery] that were almost an order of magnitude lower than the strains required to mechanically disrupt it. We conclude that under normal circumstances, a single typical (high-velocity/low amplitude) SMT thrust is very unlikely to mechanically disrupt the VA." That's certainly true. It is unlikely. Under normal circumstances. But it does happen.

They tell us that the stroke would have happened anyway. Maybe. We don't have any way of knowing. But when the patient collapses immediately after the neck is twisted, I think we can say the stroke wouldn't have happened at that time without the manipulation. Given a choice of sooner or later, later is good.

They tell us that other treatments for neck pain, like NSAIDs [nonsteroidal anti-inflammatory drugs, such as aspirin], also carry dangers. Patients have developed bleeding ulcers and died from taking aspirin. That's very true, but they are invoking the logical fallacy known as tu quoque: just because something else is dangerous too, that doesn't make neck manipulation any less dangerous. And comparing the dangers of two treatments doesn't mean there aren't other options that are safer than either of them.

Until really good studies are done, we simply don't know the magnitude of the risk; but we are reasonably

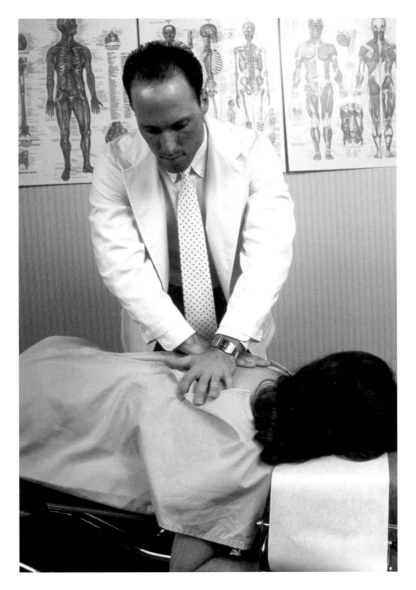

A chiropractor adjusts a patient's spine. According to one estimate, 20 percent of strokes of a particular type are caused by chiropractic adjustment of the neck. (© Art Stein/Photo Researchers, Inc.)

confident there is a risk. Now, let's measure that risk against the benefits. Some chiropractors are doing neck adjustments on 90% of their patients for everything from ear infections to low back pain. There are lots of testimonials, but no POEMS (patient-oriented evidence that matters) and no evidence of any long-term benefit or any advantage over other treatments. The only thing neck manipulations have been shown to help with is mechanical neck pain, and a recent Cochrane review did not find that manipulation was any better than simple mobilization treatments. If there is no benefit, isn't any degree of risk too much?

Other Treatment Options Are Available

There are plenty of other options for treating mechanical neck pain for those who prefer not to take pain pills. The cervical spine can be gently mobilized with physical therapy methods that have not been linked to stroke. Heat, massage, tincture of time, exercises and other measures may offer symptomatic relief with no associated risks.

"Don't ever let a chiropractor touch your neck" is the safest advice; but we can't expect everyone to accept it. Some patients have had good experiences with neck manipulations and will continue to ask for them. We can't presume to dictate to others. If someone judges that there is a one in a million risk of a stroke and is willing to take that risk, he has every right to do so. I think people have the right to engage in risky behaviors like skydiving and smoking cigarettes. I just think they deserve to know there is a risk, and to have some idea how much of a risk it is. I suspect the general public doesn't know the facts about neck manipulation. I wonder if Laurie Jean Mathiason knew neck manipulations could cause strokes. This 20 year old girl had a tailbone injury and sought out a chiropractor who manipulated her neck. Yes, her neck—to fix her tailbone! She fell into a coma and died three days later. Her visit to the chiropractor . . . in my opinion . . . qualifies as a tragedy and a crime.

Chiropractic Adjustments Do Not Cause Strokes

Christopher Kent

Christopher Kent is a chiropractor, attorney, cofounder of Chiropractic Leadership Alliance, and former chair of the United Nations NGO (Non-governmental Organization) Health Committee. He was named the International Chiropractors Association (ICA) Chiropractic Researcher of the Year in 1991 and the ICA Chiropractor of the Year in 1998. In the following viewpoint Kent claims that the fact that strokes sometimes follow chiropractic adjustments does not mean that the adjustment caused the stroke. He says that it is a logical error to confuse correlation with causation; that is, one event following another does not mean that the second event was caused by the first. According to the author, studies show that the incidence of strokes occurring after chiropractic treatments is no greater than chance. He argues that since there is no scientific evidence that adjustments cause stroke, it is not appropriate to require chiropractors to disclose such a risk to patients.

SOURCE: Christopher Kent, "Strokes: Causalities and Logical Fallacies," *Dynamic Chiropractic,* vol. 28, no. 7, March 26, 2010. dynamicchiropractic.com. Copyright © 2010 by MPA Media. All rights reserved. Reproduced by permission.

T wenty three years ago, while trying to fall asleep, I turned my head to one side. The right side of my body went numb and the room started swirling. I remember the ambulance ride and the sheer panic of not being able to feel or move my arms and legs.

After arriving at the emergency room, I had a CT [computed tomography] scan to check for a possible hemorrhage. Lying in the intensive care unit, a mechanical ventilator maintained my respiration. People I hadn't seen for years came to visit. The attending neurologist had told my family that I would probably not make it through the next few days, and that if they wanted to see me, they had better come immediately.

I recall the amalgam of horror, anger and helplessness, but most of all, a compulsion to answer the question, "Why did this happen?" Thankfully, there is a happy ending. I was visited by two chiropractors who adjusted me. Shortly after the first adjustment, I could wiggle the fingers on my right hand. Soon I was off the ventilator and able to use a wheelchair. With the unofficial consent of the attending physician, I continued to receive chiropractic adjustments while undergoing an intensive regimen of rehabilitation. A little over a month after being carried in, I walked out on my own power with the aid of a cane.

Since then, I have taught at a chiropractic college, qualified as an attorney, and co-founded a successful business. I'm again able to drive a car and pilot a light airplane. I don't consider myself a victim. And despite some residual health issues, I'm no longer seeking someone or something to blame.

Logical Fallacies

Yes, I am a stroke patient, and there is absolutely no doubt in my mind that had the event occurred while I was on a chiropractic table rather than lying in bed, the stroke would have been attributed to receiving chiro-

The author argues that because there is no scientific evidence that chiropractic adjustments cause strokes, it is not appropriate to require chiropractors to warn patients of such a risk. (© **ClassicStock/Alamy**)

practic care. Since then, I've read the accounts that have appeared in the popular media suggesting that "chiropractic manipulation" of the cervical spine is associated with strokes. I've also reviewed all of the literature that I could that has addressed the purported relationship between chiropractic cervical adjustments and strokes.

A common error in logic is equating correlation with cause and effect. The *post hoc* fallacy is the mistaken belief that because one event follows another, the first event caused the second event. This fallacy is the basis for many logical errors and superstitions. Examples range from the conclusion that bad luck follows a black cat crossing one's path, to the conclusion that if you have a heart attack within months of reading a newspaper, that reading newspapers causes heart attacks.

Consider the application of this logical fallacy to the issue of chiropractic adjustments and strokes. In a survey, neurologists were asked the number of patients evaluated over the preceding two years who suffered a neurologic complication within 24 hours of receiving a "chiropractic manipulation." Fifty-five strokes were reported. The author stated, "Patients, physicians, and chiropractors should be aware of the risk of neurologic complications associated with chiropractic manipulation."

What's wrong with this? Even if we accept unconfirmed survey results as accurate, let's change "chiropractic manipulation" to "automobile accidents." Would it be reasonable to suggest that if in 55 of the estimated millions of patient visits to chiropractors over a two-year period, a car accident resulted within 24 hours of the visit, that chiropractic adjustments cause vehicular collisions? Want to see how absurd this can get? Change "chiropractic manipulation" to chili consumption or attempted sleep, both of which occurred the night of my stroke.

A Lack of Evidence

Is there anything that would either strengthen or weaken a case of alleged causality? Yes. We can compare the number of times the event in question (in this case, stroke) occurs as a random event to the number of times the event occurs following the putative causative event (in this case, a "chiropractic manipulation"). Nearly 14 years ago, in a letter to the editor of *JMPT* [*Journal of Manipulative and Physiological Therapeutics*] [L.] Myler posed an interesting question: "I was curious how the risk of fatal stroke after cervical manipulation, placed at 0.00025%, compared with the risk of (fatal) stroke in the general population of the United States. According to data obtained from the National Center for Health Statistics, the mortality rate from stroke was calculated to be 0.00057%." But is Myler's data credible? His 0.00025% figure is from a paper by [V.] Dabbs and [W.J.] Lauretti. Their estimate is probably as good as any, since the basis for it was a reasonably comprehensive review of literature. [P.] Jaskoviak reported that not a single case of vertebral artery stroke occurred in approximately 5 million cervical "manipulations" at the National College of Chiropractic Clinic from 1965 to 1980. Not one.

A recent study by Cassidy, et al., was described in the Canadian newspaper *Globe and Mail*. The article, titled, "Chiropractors Don't Raise Stroke Risk, Study Says," reported that "Researchers say patients are no more likely to suffer a stroke following a visit to a chiropractor than they would after stepping into their family doctor's office."

The illusory concept of the risk of "chiropractic manipulation" and stroke should be considered in the context of the *de facto* standard for health care safety—allopathic medicine. In an article in the *Journal of the American Medical Association*, [C.M.] Kilo and [E.B.] Larson describe the real issues surrounding our current health care crisis: "On balance, the data remain imprecise, and the benefits that US health care currently deliver may not outweigh the aggregate health harm it imparts . . . it is time to address the possibility of net health harm by elucidating more fully aggregate health benefits and harms of current health care." In a review of errors in medicine, [L.] Leape reported that if the results of the papers reviewed were applied to the U.S. as a whole, "180,000 die each year partly as a result of iatrogenic [caused by medical examination or treatment] injury, the equivalent of three jumbo-jet crashes every 2 days."

While it is human nature to attempt to attribute a catastrophic health event to a specific cause, it must be

> **FAST FACT**
>
> A 2006 report by the National Chiropractic Mutual Insurance Company found a rate of stroke among clients given chiropractic neck manipulation of two per one hundred thousand—the same as that in the general population.

Number of Events per 10 Million People in the United States

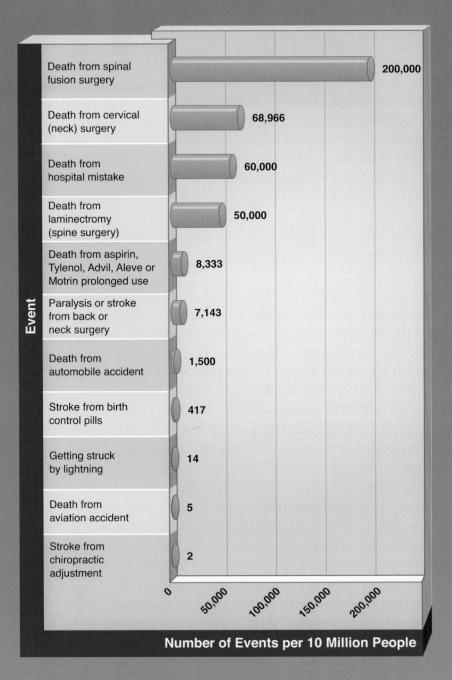

Event	Number of Events per 10 Million People
Death from spinal fusion surgery	200,000
Death from cervical (neck) surgery	68,966
Death from hospital mistake	60,000
Death from laminectromy (spine surgery)	50,000
Death from aspirin, Tylenol, Advil, Aleve or Motrin prolonged use	8,333
Paralysis or stroke from back or neck surgery	7,143
Death from automobile accident	1,500
Stroke from birth control pills	417
Getting struck by lightning	14
Death from aviation accident	5
Stroke from chiropractic adjustment	2

Taken from: Philip Greenwood. "The Safety of Chiropractic." Greenwood Chiropractic. www.thegreenwoodcenter.com /chirosafe.php.

remembered that the mere fact that one event follows another does not mean that the first caused the second. There is no scientific evidence establishing a causal relationship between stroke and chiropractic adjustments. Superstition, speculation, and logical fallacies should not form the basis for public policy or informed consent. Any attempt to mandate a disclosure of such a putative relationship, in my opinion, is utterly inappropriate.

Poor and Disadvantaged Patients Are Not Getting the Help They Need

Kristi L. Kirschner

Kristi L. Kirschner is a rehabilitation physician at Schwab Rehabilitation Hospital and a professor of medical humanities and bioethics and of physical medicine and rehabilitation at Northwestern University. In the following viewpoint Kirschner argues that the poor and uninsured face many challenges that make stroke more likely, and if they have a stroke, they are unable to access the treatment and rehabilitation services they require. She claims that poor and uninsured people who have health factors that make stroke more likely, such as diabetes and hypertension, are much less likely to have those conditions diagnosed before a stroke occurs. Kirschner also says that it is very difficult for an uninsured stroke patient to get rehabilitation services during the critical first three months after a stroke. According to Kirschner, health care reform is needed that emphasizes preventive measures and takes into account psychological, environmental, and social aspects of health care.

SOURCE: Kristi L. Kirschner, "One City, Two Worlds," *The Hastings Center Report,* September–October 2010, pp. 6–7. Copyright © 2010 by The Hastings Center. All rights reserved. Reproduced by permission.

The scenario is becoming achingly familiar to me: a woman in her fifties with no health insurance suffers a stroke. With luck, it is a small stroke—a "warning sign." But the patients I'm likely to see as a rehabilitation physician are usually not that lucky. The stroke is invariably large, causing significant disability. And the other familiar part of this scene? While treating her, I discover, unbeknownst to the patient, that her blood sugar and blood pressure are out of control. Undoubtedly, the undiagnosed hypertension and diabetes contributed to the stroke.

So what's the back story? Perhaps she works a job that doesn't provide insurance, or she can't afford the premiums. She has mouths to feed, rent to pay, and bills. She's raising her children in a violent neighborhood where the public schools are inferior, receiving a little over half of the tax dollars per student that the wealthier suburban schools do. She takes three buses to get to work. Her neighborhood has no grocery stores with healthy food, only fast food and liquor stores. Preventive health care is not an option.

The acute care hospital where the uninsured person is admitted immediately starts the process of applying for public aid. The process takes about three months—the initial months most critical for stroke rehabilitation—and in the meantime, finding an acute inpatient rehabilitation facility willing to accept a patient who is "public aid pending" is extremely difficult. Once the public aid is in place, medical options will be a little easier to find—but only a little. Fewer doctors accept public aid. An elective procedure—like a knee replacement for crippling arthritis—is almost unattainable for many public aid patients.

Psychological, Social, and Environmental Aspects of Health Care

After working on Chicago's upscale Gold Coast for twenty-two years, I recently moved my clinical practice to the

Lawndale community, one of Chicago's poorest. I joined Schwab Rehabilitation Hospital, part of the Sinai Health System. Though they are only five miles apart, the neighborhoods and the health care systems couldn't be more different.

Since I first learned about George Engel's biopsychosocial model of medicine in medical school twenty-five years ago and throughout my following years practicing physiatry [rehabilitation medicine], I've been increasingly convinced that such a heuristic [technique] best captures the scope of the problems (and potential solutions) in health care. A core principle for rehabilitation physicians is that disability is a product of both the patient and the environment. An expanded notion of this principle is now being captured in the "biopsychoecological model," which adds an environmental perspective to the social domain. I think about my young stroke patient from Lawndale in this context. She may be impaired from her stroke, but her mobility difficulties are exacerbated by lack of a wheelchair-accessible home, curb cuts, and safe public transportation systems. The environment is absolutely critical to her health and well-being, as are her medications, an appropriate diet, personal assistant services, and health care professionals who accept public aid. While these issues are not unique to Lawndale and can arise on the Gold Coast as well, the pervasiveness, scope, and severity of these issues are exponentially worse for those in the former community.

So here I am—thinking more about these basic needs than whether the Lokomat [a robot-assisted treadmill] or robotic therapy is the best treatment for my patient's hemiparesis [weakness on one side of the body]. I'm lucky because my current hospital system is one of the few that provides rehabilitation services for patients who are

FAST FACT

Twenty-five percent of stroke patients stopped taking one or more of their medications within several months, *Archives of Neurology* reported in 2011. Reasons given included financial difficulty and lack of insurance.

"public aid pending," but what about her medications, medical supplies, and needed equipment? What about transportation to and from appointments? And how to get her timely, adequate personal assistant services? This latter is particularly critical as her daughter—the first of her family to attend college—is considering dropping out of school to take care of her mom. The only other viable alternative—a urine-soaked, short-staffed nursing home—is simply too heartbreaking to consider.

Community Health Interventions

The Sinai Urban Health Institute [SUHI] is also part of the Sinai Health System, along with Schwab Rehabilitation Hospital. Established in 1990, SUHI initially used community epidemiological methods, going door to

An uninsured young stroke victim is comforted in a rehab clinic by a friend. Uninsured stroke victims are at greater risk because they typically cannot afford proper care in the first three months after a stroke, the most important time to start rehabilitation. (© AP Images/Brian Kersey)

door to map the surrounding neighborhoods. It discovered that a person in North Lawndale can expect to live a full seven years less than the average Chicagoan, and that obesity, violence, hypertension, diabetes, and asthma are rampant. It has since developed and piloted several community health interventions, such as a pediatric asthma initiative called "Healthy Home, Healthy Child." This program provides in-home visits from community health educators, who help to identify and eliminate asthma triggers like mold, mice, household pets, cigarette smoke, cockroaches, and cleaning products. They also reinforce the proper use of asthma medications and

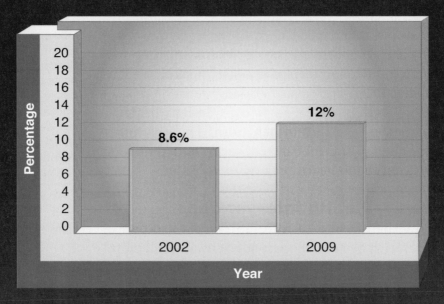

Percentage of Stroke Patients Not Taking Prescribed Medicine Due to Cost, 2002 and 2009

Taken from: Michelle G. Sullivan. "More Struggle to Pay for Drugs Post Stroke." *Internal Medicine News*, vol. 44, no. 4, March 1, 2011, p.1.

treatments. Such programs are producing impressive benefits, including dramatic decreases in the number of emergency room visits, hospital admissions, and use of urgent health care services. For this work on asthma, SUHI was recently honored by the Environmental Protection Agency and the American Hospital Association. It is now carrying out similar community-based initiatives in a number of other areas, including diabetes, obesity, breast cancer, and HIV/AIDS.

Programs like these are somewhat counterintuitive for hospital administrations. Hospitals get paid to have patients in them, not to keep them out. They cater to privately insured patients receiving expensive procedures, not to patients with chronic illnesses and difficult social problems who are on public aid and have no health insurance. They don't like to spend a lot of money on interpreter services (for which insurance does not reimburse) for populations who don't speak English as a primary language. Nor do they want to spend time and resources focusing on the needs of patients who can't afford their medications or qualify for home health care or get transportation services to and from the hospital. And yet, somehow, SUHI and the Sinai Hospital Systems are committed to all these things. The good news is that such community-based and hospital service programs can work very well. The bad news is that these programs are often pilot projects, and the resources and infrastructure to sustain them are extremely challenging to attain when the donor or research funding runs out.

Determinants of Health

In 2009, as I was pondering my career move and how I wanted to focus my time and energy over the next phase of my life, I had the chance to hear one of my mentors, Dr. James Webster, give the commencement address to the Northwestern University Feinberg School of Medicine. He said:

In terms of the determinants of health, remember that genes are responsible for about one-third of what happens to each of us. Even with what we learn daily about genomics and how we can use individual patient information to guide some of our therapeutics, there is little that we can do to alter genetic complement at the present time. Surprisingly, medical care accounts for only about 15 percent of health outcomes. I know that you will take care of this to perfection. It is the other 50 percent of determinants of health that I want you to address on a daily basis. This involves the behavioral choices that account for a third of how long and how well people live. What they eat and drink, how much they, or we, exercise, whether or not individuals smoke or use other addictive drugs, how obese our country becomes. . . .

The real killers are cigarettes, obesity, inactivity, diet, alcohol, preventable infectious diseases, guns, and motor vehicle accidents.

These words ring true to me. I am fascinated by the biological aspects of medicine and as hopeful for the possibilities of regenerative medicine and designer drugs as anyone. But as I continued to work on the Gold Coast and see the best medical care money can buy, I increasingly felt out of balance. Just as our health care system is disproportionately weighted to high-tech, rarified downstream interventions for those who can pay, so was I. It was time for me to right my internal balance, as well as contribute to the larger social rebalancing that we so desperately need. And therein lies my hope: that the movement to health care reform will embrace and value the work of such places as Sinai, that my next patient can get access to health care and social services before she has a debilitating stroke, and that we can recognize that health care is inextricably linked to psychological, social, and environmental issues and invest accordingly in these domains. Only time will tell if my hopes are a pipedream, but for now I'm excited to be a part of a team working to make them a reality.

CHAPTER 3

Living with Stroke

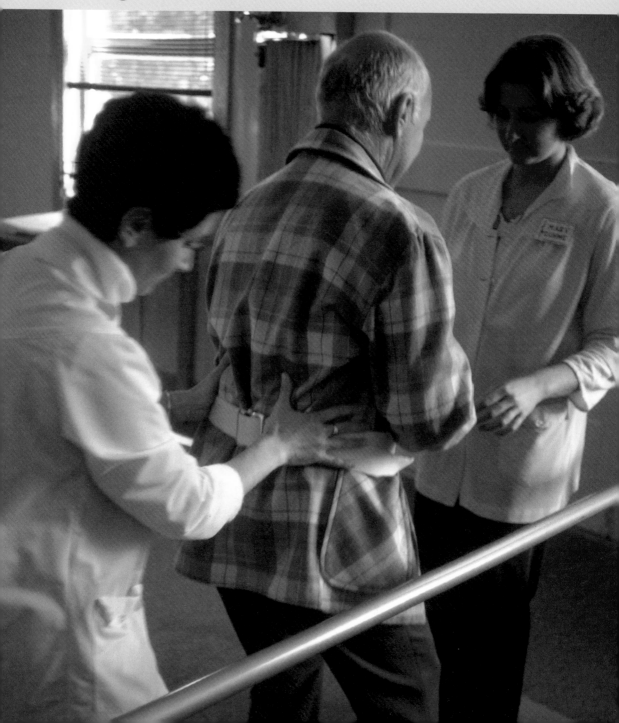

A Thirty-Eight-Year-Old Mother Tells the Story of Her Stroke

Kinan K. Hreib

S.H. is the mother of two young children. In the following viewpoint she tells the story of the stroke she had at the age of thirty-eight, including her visit to the emergency room, the reaction of her husband and children to her stroke, her rehabilitation, and how her family and friends finally came to accept her new reality. Her story appears as "A Patient's Perspective" in Kinan K. Hreib's book *100 Questions and Answers About Stroke: A Lahey Clinic Guide*.

Last year, at the age of 38, I had a stroke. I thought strokes happened to old people; I was young and healthy with two young children. One day after a short jog, I developed a headache. I had had headaches before, but this new headache was different: It was on the right side of my head and more severe than usual. I was concerned, but because I have had headaches that sub-

Photo on previous page. A stroke victim rehabilitates through balance training. Recovery from stroke is usually a long and arduous process. (© Josephus Daniels/ Photo Researchers, Inc.)

SOURCE: Kinan K. Hreib, *100 Questions and Answers About Stroke: A Lahey Clinic Guide*, Sudbury, MA: Jones and Bartlett Publishers, 2009, pp. ix–xii. Copyright © 2009 by Jones & Bartlett Learning, www.jblearning.com. All rights reserved. Reproduced by permission.

PERSPECTIVES ON DISEASES AND DISORDERS

sided before, I had a sense of false comfort. I kept saying to myself, this headache will go away like all the others. I should have listened to my inside voice telling me something was wrong.

I should have listened, but I decided to find a more comforting explanation. The next morning the headache continued, becoming more severe. I took some Tylenol and drove the kids to school, as I usually do. The children knew something was not right. My daughter asked me if I was feeling okay. Later that day I collapsed to the floor, not able to move the left side of my body. I did not know what happened. I had a feeling that it had something to do with my headache. I tried to get up to reach the phone. All I could think about was who was going to get the children from school, feed them dinner, and help them with their homework. I crawled slowly on the floor until I reached the telephone, pulled the telephone down to the floor, and called for help. The emergency medical technicians arrived within 10 minutes. During those 10 minutes I called my husband and told him about the problems I was having; he was having a hard time understanding me, and I realized I had a problem with my speech. He knew there was something wrong.

Going to the Emergency Room

I was taken to the emergency room of a local hospital, and my husband, Tom, arrived half an hour later. I was confused and didn't know what had happened, and my husband was clearly panicked, trying to find a doctor to talk to, wanting answers quickly. I could hear my husband screaming at the nurses and doctors; he was tearful and scared. I tried to move. I wanted to get up and walk away from this nightmare, but I couldn't. I started crying, and my left arm and leg were not moving. I felt helpless. I had a great life and family and I was healthy. What had happened? Why me, God? Why me? Did I do something wrong to deserve this? Can somebody help me?

I heard sounds in the background. People were running around, some talking to me and others not. Someone was taking blood from my arm while another person was putting a needle in my other arm. I knew they were talking to me and I could hear them, but in my state of absolute panic I could not focus. I tried to talk; my speech was slow and difficult to understand. I looked in the eyes of the doctors and nurses for answers. I wanted to make sure they saw me. I was trying to read their faces. What is going on with me? Please tell me. The doctors were asking questions about my symptoms. I tried to answer, hoping that my answers would help them with the diagnosis. One of them finally said he thought I was having a stroke. I am not sure I fully comprehended what he said to me. As they wheeled me to the scanner, I began thinking of how a stroke could affect me. I have seen people with stroke; some were in bad shape. Some could not talk or eat on their own; some could not walk or use their arm. What's going to happen to my children? Did I cause the stroke? What's going to happen to me? Please, God, give me another chance.

My husband followed me to the scanner. I could see his tears, but I don't think he talked— he probably didn't know what to say. The scan took less than 5 minutes. I was hoping the doctors were wrong and that when the scan was done I could just walk off the stretcher and out of the emergency room, back to my comfortable home with my children. I finally asked Tom about the kids. He told me they were with their grandmother and were okay. One of the doctors walked in to tell me that the CT [computed tomography scan] was normal. For a few seconds I felt relieved that there was no stroke. But the doctor then explained that the CT may not detect the stroke and that he and his team of other doctors believed that I had experienced a stroke. Before I could ask whether they could do something to help me,

FAST FACT

According to the American Stroke Association, stroke is more common in men than women, but more than half of all stroke deaths occur in women. At all ages, more women than men die of stroke.

the doctor was telling me about a drug that could possibly help my stroke. My mind was racing; I don't think I heard everything the doctor said.

A Risky Treatment

Now I know that he talked to me and my husband about t-PA [tissue plasminogen activator]. He told us the drug was not effective in all cases and that it may kill me. For a moment I thought the doctor had the answer, but even in my shocked state I could tell the treatment was risky and that the doctor was uncertain about the treatment. I later learned that giving t-PA is not straightforward. I wanted something to help me; I really wanted to go back home; I did not want my kids to see me like this. Tom believed that the drug was risky, but I said I wanted to receive it. I received the medication while in the emergency room, but my symptoms did not go away. I felt desperate, but I was also very tired. I fell asleep until the next morning.

The next day my husband and my children came to visit. My daughter cried and looked terrified. My son was composed but very uncomfortable. He did not want to hug me and sat far away from the bed. After my family left I felt lonely. I wished there were someone with me just to tell me that it was going to be okay. A whole bunch of doctors came in to talk to me. They asked me to do things with my left arm, but I couldn't. However, my left leg was moving. I smiled at the first glimmer of hope, a small victory perhaps. I wanted some feedback from the doctors, and one of them said the movement was a good sign. I had not had anything to eat in more than 24 hours, but I wasn't hungry. The doctor told me they would do more tests to figure out what caused the stroke, and they would also test my swallowing before I was allowed to eat. For the next few days I stayed in the hospital. I wanted to leave, but I knew I could not take care of myself or my children. I started feeling desperate again. I was hoping that I would regain strength and be back to normal by now, but only my leg was moving.

I didn't even know if my leg was strong enough to stand on. My swallowing was fine, so I was allowed to eat. I must have been hungry because the hospital food tasted good. My family visited every day, and by the third day my son gave me a hug and sat next to me, stroking my head. From that moment on I knew that no matter what deficits I had that I was still loved and that the stroke had not taken away my motherhood or who I was to my family.

Rehabilitation

Finally, I was discharged to a rehabilitation hospital where I stayed for almost 2 months. During that time I worked hard to stand up with help and then independently. Strength in my left arm slowly improved, but my hand remained weak. My speech went back to normal. While at the rehabilitation hospital I was treated for depression and for some pain that I developed in my left shoulder. My husband, family, and friends visited me every day. I got to know my family, and my family got to know me in a different way. I found my family to be very supportive, and I saw the compassion of strangers. Many other people with stroke, young and old, became my friends. Age didn't seem to be an obstacle: We shared the same problems, we had the same pain, we all walked "funny," and some talked like drunks. Some days were more depressing than others, but I knew that I had a family waiting for me. The 2 months in rehabilitation were the longest 2 months of my life, and the most painful, but at the end of it, I felt more alive. Humpty Dumpty was back together, scarred but definitely alive.

My self-employed husband stopped working for almost 3 months. We depleted our savings and had to borrow money. Now, almost 1 year after the stroke I am still not back to normal, but I have stopped feeling sorry for myself. I force myself to get out of bed every day. I get tired quickly, but I take a nap and then do more. I tried jogging again but the spastic leg and joint pains made this difficult. I am now a great swimmer. Being in the pool

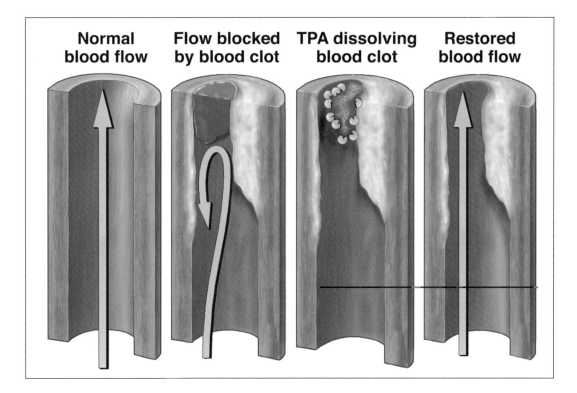

Normal blood flow — **Flow blocked by blood clot** — **TPA dissolving blood clot** — **Restored blood flow**

takes the weight off my joints, and I can still get a workout without too much pain.

I know that I have a purpose. I speak to support groups and anyone who is willing to listen about my stroke. I tell people who suffered from stroke not to give up. I did not realize how slow my recovery would be, and I did not realize what can happen to the body after a stroke or how my stroke was going to affect people around me. My immediate family went through a period of grief at my apparent loss. I grieved too for my lost self, but my family and I learned to like the new me. I have a different perspective on life. My life was turned upside down in only a few hours and a year later I am still not right-side-up, but I no longer think of the events as a big tragedy. I don't know what made me feel better and start to recover, but I know that my family gave me a purpose to work hard and recover.

Tissue plasminogen activator (TPA, also tPA and t-PA) is a drug that unclots arteries to restore blood flow, as shown in this illustration. Its use in the treatment of stroke is risky. (© **Nucleus Medical Art, Inc./Alamy**)

A Woman Cares for Her Husband After His Stroke

Maureen Duffin-Ward and Michael Ward

Maureen Duffin-Ward is the author of *Suddenly Southern: A Yankee's Guide to Living in Dixie.* She is married to Michael Ward, a former television executive who suffered a massive stroke that left him severely incapacitated. Duffin-Ward describes the challenges of becoming a caretaker to her formerly capable husband and adapting to their very different post-stroke lives together.

"Aardvark," I say.

"Art fart," he says after me.

"Aaarddddd . . ." I lay on the d.

"Fart"

I pull up Google Images, and my computer is a visual display of the absurdity of it all. "Look, Michael," I say

SOURCE: Maureen Duffin-Ward and Michael Ward, "An A to Z Survivors' Guide by the Most Reliable Source in Stroke Recovery— Someone Who's Been There," *Topics in Stroke Rehabilitation*, vol. 18, no. 2, 2011, pp. 139–143. Copyright © 2011 by THOMAS LAND PUBLISHERS. All rights reserved. Reproduced with permission of THOMAS LAND PUBLISHERS in the format Other book and Textbook via Copyright Clearance Center.

laughing as I show him the crazy creatures. "There aren't a lot of aardvarks in Washington, DC, let's move on to the next one."

And then I get the look that requires no words. That reprimand over the reading glasses familiar to anyone who plays around when there's work to be done, a glance Michael perfected as a high-level television executive so eloquent with words he was asked to testify before Congress on behalf of broadcast television stations. He now has expressive aphasia, but he still knows how to make a point that will bring you around to his side.

"This is very important to me," he says.

"Aardvark," I say, this time like I mean it.

"Aardvark," he repeats with triumph.

No Typical Days

Before his stroke, Michael was the news director for a Washington, DC, television station, so he's used to business plans. And now he's all about the business of getting better. He presented his plan today: "Learn to read the dictionary and get smarter everyday." It's been 19 months since his massive stroke, yet we're back at the beginning again, and that's how recovery works. It's as if you're on a train that moves forward and backward so you never get to your destination. Sometimes you like the ride, and sometimes you just want to get off.

People often ask me what a typical day is like. But typical days are something you have before the stroke. When one day your brilliant husband is learning to talk and one day he's learning to walk, when a microwave is too high-tech for a gadget guru who repaired his own motherboards, when the former president of a television station can no longer read or write, there's no such thing as a typical day.

I was a sales manager for NBC in Philadelphia when this big hotshot from our Chicago station was introduced as a new vice president. He shook my hand, and an electric jolt went through my body. I walked away thinking, "What was that?"

It was (and is) the love of my life. Michael proposed on the second date, and we were married within 6 months. We just knew. And 15 years later, we still do.

I have never looked up to or loved anyone more. In addition to leading a Chicago newsroom from fourth to first place and winning local Emmy's [television awards] and Addy's [advertising awards] and accolades all over the country, Michael was a low 80s golfer, a gorgeous gardener, and a professional photographer—there was absolutely nothing he couldn't do. As much as I admired his individual talents, it was the sheer quantity of skills that dazzled me more. He drove cross-country in blizzards and hurricanes and read a map like [explorers] Lewis and Clark. A big sports fan, he loved comparing notes with other fans (when he was a photojournalist, he had his camera in one hand and caught a fly ball with the other at a Cleveland Tribe game), and he'd be just as excited talking Civil War battles with a history buff or art history with a curator. His rock and roll band from back in the day was just inducted into the South Dakota Hall of Fame. He could fix anything around the house and, yep, design the floor plans, too. Yet, Michael always made me feel like the catch. And that spoiling has served him well. Because now when Michael wants to go for a ride (he can no longer drive himself, so Driving Mr. Daisy it is); when he smiles and says, "Say . . . wanna go for a swim?" (my long ago lifeguard uses all his strength just to get in the pool); when he points to his newspaper and asks me to "read him a few bars"; when he needs me to cut his toenails or requires help in the bathroom all I have to do is flash back and remember. I don't think he ever said no to me.

The Role of Caregiver

The role of the caregiver is huge. It's relentless. And while I have enjoyed some of the richest moments of my life after the stroke, I would be doing a huge disservice to all survivors and caretakers if I did not speak the truth.

A stroke is brutal. When Michael came home from the hospital, he could not speak, read, or write and that was just the beginning of our troubles. He was incontinent. That gleam in his eyes when I walked into a room was gone. The guy who laughed first and laughed hardest at all my jokes was not amused. My confidante and advisor who coached me when life got hard was now my biggest difficulty. He couldn't shower without assist, and when he insisted on doing it himself (growling no less), he fell when I left the room. He didn't know how to work his electric razor, and he needed me to shave him. It looked like something out of Psycho [the suspense film containing a bloody shower scene] in our bathroom. (I don't recommend the Lady Bic [disposable shaver] for someone on blood thinners who is hairy like [the] Unabomber.) He needed help dressing. He couldn't eat his meal without dropping the utensils, and cutting his food was my job. He couldn't turn on his computer. He couldn't work his iPod. He couldn't handle money. He no longer knew how to work his remote. (I never did.) The man who could do everything, couldn't do anything. He combed his underarm hair instead of the hair on his head. My go-to guy was gone.

> **FAST FACT**
>
> A 2009 study published in *Stroke* found that over 90 percent of stroke caregivers felt their caregiving role increased their appreciation of life, and 81 percent felt more strong and confident.

It's surreal when you're discharged from the hospital. Impossible to fathom you're on your own. There's this huge disconnect between you and the powers-that-be who say you're ready for home. To be fair, the hospital staff/insurance company compared Michael to when he arrived (near dead), so they were pleased with his before and after. We had a different before and after in mind, so we were nothing short of horrified with extreme makeover: disability addition.

"Michael made a cup of coffee today," said his occupational therapist days before discharge.

"Seriously? He made coffee?" I was highly doubtful knowing his new skill set.

"Well, he forgot the water . . ."

Um, with all due respect to occupational therapists, that's not making coffee. That's making a fire. Don't try that at home.

But of course, he did. And watching him try to fill the carafe with his left hand (his once dominant right dangling forgotten by his side), measure his coffee counting "one, eight, eleven," drool running down his chin because he was concentrating so hard, didn't conjure up a barista. But I had to relax. Okay, not relax, but not have his 'n her strokes with every cup of Joe.

A Good Support Team

Slowly, and I mean slowly, we found our way. We couldn't have done it without the kindness, compassion, and unwavering support we receive from Michael's medical team. I love Michael's primary doc, the one after the stroke, and I adore the neurologists at George Washington University Hospital who saved Michael's life.

But it's rehab (in our case outpatient speech rehab specifically) that shapes the quality of the life that's been saved. Thanks to divine intervention (a television anchor/former colleague shared our case with a board member at National Rehabilitation Hospital [NRH]), Michael and I found ourselves in the inimitable care of Patty and Paul at NRH in Washington, DC.

Michael was a man of few words when he was discharged from the hospital. He had global aphasia—scoring FIM [functional independence measure] 1, the lowest of the low, so speech therapy was our lifeline. Talk about a team effort. Patty and Paul double-teamed Michael, and they double-teamed me. They not only taught Michael how to talk after the stroke, but they also taught me how to listen. They had this magical way of making me a part of it, even when my part was staying home. Michael loved owning his lessons, and I absolutely adored the break. It was the only time I ever felt he was in better hands than mine. Patty and Paul would call me with progress reports, and they didn't talk in FIMs; their enthusiasm was contagious. "He was a rock star today," "He called a restaurant CHIC!" I loved hearing the results at home, too.

I heard Michael practicing on the couch, "More, More, Maur-een," I don't know who was more excited when he finally spit it out (Michael, Patty, or I), but it was the first time he'd said my name in 5 months and it was worth the wait. And that's not the biggest payoff from speech therapy.

A Small Victory

For months after the stroke, Michael was trying to tell me someone owed him money. Since most of the handouts were all in the family, I just waved him off. But he kept trying another way to get it across. Think Charades when your partner can't get any of the clues. One day he wrote down $12,000.

"Someone owes you twelve thousand dollars?" I asked, thinking it was like my birthday when he said I could spend "300 million."

"YES!" he said, with such force that I believed him.

He marched into his study and was clearly dismayed to see I had cleaned his desk. (And by clean, I mean I tossed it all in a trash bag and threw it out. I was overwhelmed by all the paper.)

"Rats," he said softly, drawing out every letter.

"What are you looking for?"

"Back."

He was rifling through his briefcase. Somehow I figured out he was looking for his day planner (book). Last year's to be exact. I retrieved it from another room and handed it to him. He paged to July and pointed to the date where he'd written "Adorama/$12,000." I Googled

Adorama, and it was a camera shop in New York. I was beyond excited with my guess: "You sold your cameras before the stroke, and you never got paid!!!!!!"

It was like the world champs of Charades. He hugged me. We were jumping up and down. But not as high as we jumped 2 weeks later when the $12,000 check arrived.

It's like life on steroids. The good stuff is so much better, and the bad stuff is so much worse.

Recovery Never Ends

They say if you don't get it back in the first year, it's probably not coming back. Ask any stroke survivor and they will tell you they continue to improve forever. But in year 1, you learn to walk and talk again; whereas year 2, the improvements aren't quite as dramatic. Adding aardvark to your vocabulary isn't as big as the first time a survivor walks to Starbucks by himself, orders hot chocolate, hands over the right money, and leaves his wife at home. I admit to cheating the first time, calling ahead to tell them what he would order, but then I learned to let go.

Michael is back. Not my prestroke Michael who could do it all, but our huge connection survived after all. We laugh, we learn, we love. And when all else fails, we hug. You haven't been serenaded until someone with aphasia sings "Happy Trails" to you as you fall off to sleep.

I will never ever stop missing the Michael before the stroke; I will never stop missing being in the passenger seat of the best driven car; I will never stop missing his computer assist, his great mind at work, his take on politics, on life, on people. But there's one thing I'll never have to miss. The enormous power of true love. He promises me he'll come all the way back. I'm not sure about that, but it's an honor to have his back.

A Sister's Perspective on the Aftermath of a Stroke

Stephanie Tames

Stephanie Tames is a writer and yoga instructor. In the following viewpoint she describes how her sister's stroke strained their relationship and put a burden on the health care system. Tames says that although she feels obligated to help, her sister's level of need is overwhelming.

The ambulance driver knows my sister's name. He's come to her apartment a dozen times, summoned there by a 911 call placed by my sister or her emergency response company. The call button hangs around her neck like the creamy strand of pearls she used to wear to work.

Not long ago she accused the driver of stealing her prescription pain medicine from her purse when he took her to the hospital. She said she didn't notice it was

SOURCE: Stephanie Tames, "The Messy, Personal Side of Health Care," *Atlanta Journal-Constitution*, January 6, 2010, p. A13. Copyright © 2010 by Stephanie Tames. All rights reserved. Reproduced by permission.

gone until after she returned home. She called the police. They've been to her apartment before, too.

Four years ago my sister had a stroke that left her speech altered and the left side of her body damaged. Now, her left arm is thinner than her right, the muscles

FAST FACT

The Centers for Disease Control and Prevention estimated the cost of stroke to the United States in 2010 at $53.9 billion, resulting from health care costs, medications, and missed workdays.

useless and withered, and the hand on that side curls in on itself like a backwards question mark. She tucks her arm close to her body and keeps her twisted hand hidden under the sleeve of the sweater she always wears. She's cautious with her arm as if it's cradling something fragile, like a baby bird.

The muscles in her left leg are weak and even when her brain is able to send it the right signals to bend, lift and step, it no longer has the ability to hold her upright. She uses a tripod cane to walk, relying on the strength of her right side to keep her body steady. Even then she battles the laws of gravity.

Overusing the Medical System

There were problems earlier, surgery for a brain aneurism that didn't go well. And before that, throughout her teen and early adult years, well, let's just say she liked to party. Still, she held good jobs, was married, has a son.

But then things started to go wrong. Divorce. Bad decisions. She fell back into old habits. Now she lives alone, relying on disability and food stamps. A home health aide gets her bathed and dressed and fixes her meals. She's broke.

My sister has a primary care doctor but often she goes to the emergency room instead. It's easier. She doesn't have to make an appointment or call for the medical van. She goes for things like a sinus infection, migraines, a pain in her back. Bronchitis. Sometimes she really needs the emergency room. Her heart is weak. She has breakthrough seizures.

But more and more she goes because they'll give her what she wants. She wants the medicines that make her numb. She wants the medicines that make her happy. She gets these from her doctor, too, but it's never enough.

It would be easy to say that my sister is part of the problem with health care, why costs are rising out of proportion to the care that's given. She overuses, and misuses, the system. Each of her unnecessary trips to the emergency room costs thousands of dollars. Medicaid is picking up the bill, which means we're picking it up through our taxes. These are the facts.

Overwhelming Neediness

But she's not alone in creating this problem. I'm part of it, too. I don't take care of my sister.

She needs rides to the doctor. That might help her stop using the emergency room as her personal physician. She needs someone to keep track of her medicines. She needs companionship. She needs money. She needs help managing her pain, and her use of pain-numbing, mind-numbing drugs.

Needs. That's the way it is with my sister and why I can't help her. She needs so much, takes so much. It's been that way for a long time. I don't know what happened. And I don't know why I feel the way I do. Maybe the strokes and her other health problems altered her in some essential way. Maybe I'm the one who changed. All I know is that I love my sister, but I can't help her.

My sister reminds me that the Bible says family should take care of one another. I know she's right. But when I help I feel like I've stepped into quicksand, her needs become its sucking hold pulling me deeper each time I try to move away. I've learned I can only give a little at a time, and to let the rest go.

The Messy Unpredictability of Life

My sister is part of the problem [that] health care costs have soared. I am, too. But don't judge us too harshly.

We didn't plan it this way. One minute we're two girls riding our bikes together. The next, four decades have passed and I'm pushing my sister in a wheelchair while she stares off into some memory, her face pulled into a crooked smile.

What my sister and I didn't know all those years ago was how messy life can be. And unpredictable. I think she'd say that if those were life's lessons, she aced them. I wouldn't disagree.

I visit my sister a couple of times a year. We talk on the phone often. I send her a little money when I can, try to help her avert one crisis or another. Should. Need. Responsibility. Care. Enough. I see these words everywhere, often like an aura hovering over my life.

On the phone my sister asks me if I remembered when we used to go dancing together at clubs. She loved to dance and had a natural rhythm that I envied. We didn't need partners. She would grab my hand and pull me onto the dance floor and I'd follow her with complete abandon. She'd throw her arms up in the air, her head falling back, and she'd shimmy and sway while I pretended that I looked just like her. On the other end of the phone, I knew she was smiling her lopsided smile and I was smiling, too. Of course I remember, I tell her. But we were different then.

A Man Describes His Recovery from a Stroke When He Was Ten Years Old

David Dow

David Dow is an inspirational speaker. He received an award from the Ohio Speech Hearing Association for his work on raising awareness for people with aphasia. In the following viewpoint Dow describes the experience of having a stroke at age ten and his subsequent struggle with aphasia, a disability that impaired his ability to speak, read, and write. Now twenty-five years old, he shares the perspective he gained over the years on the stroke recovery process.

I had a massive stroke when I was ten years old. I was living in Ohio and came to Las Vegas with my family. The trip was supposed to be 3 days, but I got home nearly 3 months later. This is my story of how I overcame many challenges over the last fifteen years so I could live a "normal" life again.

SOURCE: David Dow, "My So Called 'Normal' Life," *The Challenger Newspaper* (Las Vegas), vol. 14, no. 4, April, 2010. thechallengernews paper.com. Copyright © 2010 by *The Challenger Newspaper*. All rights reserved. Reproduced by permission.

Before my stroke I was active, outgoing, and had lots of friends. I loved school and was in the gifted program.

On the first day in Las Vegas I wasn't feeling well. My mom and I stayed back at the hotel while the others went to Zion National Park.

Shortly after they left, I had my stroke. I ended up in the Intensive Care Unit and couldn't talk, read, write, or even understand. My entire right side was paralyzed. I couldn't walk and even swallowing food was hard. I had some seizures.

I had to have two brain surgeries because of a vascular problem that caused my stroke. Once I stabilized, the hard work of rehab began.

Struggling with Aphasia

After nearly 3 months of rehab, I was finally able to go back to school. I was so excited!! But, most of the teachers and my friends didn't really understand what I was going through. I was now in a wheelchair and couldn't talk due to my aphasia. Aphasia is the disability that affected my speaking, reading, and even writing. Aphasia does not affect intellect.

I was so frustrated. Everyone treated me differently. I felt lonely, sad, and really angry. I knew inside that I had to fight to get better.

I progressed in rehab. I learned how to use my left hand for everything. (I'd been right handed) I went from the wheelchair, to walker, to cane, to walking by myself.

My aphasia was my biggest problem. I went to lots of speech therapy and my mom worked with me and she hired others to help me too. Finally, I was able to talk again—starting with just single words.

It's now been 15 years since my stroke. I am now 25. I've had years and years of speech therapy and can now

> **FAST FACT**
>
> A 2010 *New York Times* article reports an estimated rate of stroke in children under age eighteen of twelve per one hundred thousand, or approximately nine thousand strokes per year in the United States.

speak quite well. I can read and write again. I'm walking. Things aren't as easy as before, but I live independently and strive to live a "normal" life.

I will never give up. I still go to rehab in Henderson, NV where my family has moved to. I attend a stroke support group and joined in an aquatic swim class for survivors. I work out at the gym.

The Importance of Mental Stimulation

My hobbies are going to the movies, playing the Nintendo Wii as part of my therapy, and traveling. My family even organized a stroke cruise a few years ago. I went on a trip to Europe this past year by myself. For me, traveling is a good way to challenge myself and enjoy life again.

I'd like to share my thoughts on achieving goals. Stimulating the mind is important. I had lots of therapy. I was not allowed to sit in front of the TV all day. I kept busy with learning how to grow a garden, learning to watercolor paint, use educational games on the computer and more.

I believe it is impossible to recover by lying in your bed all day as you won't accomplish anything. You have to make an effort.

It is very hard work to be faced with a disability and rehab. Everything changes. It affects you emotionally, physically, and your goals can change.

Coping with this new disability is rough and it affects the people who love you too. But, eventually you will get it. Patience is important, very important.

I couldn't even talk, play soccer, or even hang out with my friends. My life had totally changed. Sometimes, I felt sad and even angry. I think it is normal to show your emotions as it's part of the healing process.

Believing in Recovery

I think having faith is crucial too. You have to believe that you will get better. It takes a strong desire to recover and work hard on it so you can. There are many obstacles, but you have to believe you can face them to overcome them.

I often had failed attempts at things I tried. But, I tried again and again. When you put your mind to it, you can go far.

I think it is important to focus on what I *can* do, not on what I can not. I still have some paralysis on my right side with my hand, ankle, and toes. I can drive and I walk without a cane. I talk, read, and write again. It isn't as easy as before.

No two strokes are alike. No two recoveries will be the same. But we all must find the motivation and courage to keep trying. There will be times you want to quit. But, you must fight to overcome the down days. You have to do what needs to be done whether you feel like it or not.

My goals have changed. I wanted to be a doctor like my dad. I think I would have been a great doctor. But, I can still help people. I want to encourage and help others with stroke and aphasia. I can still make a difference. My stroke can't take that away from me.

GLOSSARY

anosognosia	An indifference to or lack of awareness of one's deficit or disability; for example, a visually impaired stroke patient who claims he or she can still see perfectly.
aphasia	A disorder characterized by either partial or total loss of the ability to communicate, either verbally or through written words. A person with aphasia may have difficulty speaking, reading, writing, recognizing the names of objects, or understanding what other people have said.
apoplexy	*See* **stroke**
arteriovenous malformation (AVM)	A disorder in which there are abnormal connections between arteries and veins, resulting in a complex tangle of blood vessels. AVM can result in a stroke or other complications.
assistive/adaptive technology (AT)	Equipment or software used to overcome functional or communications limitations caused by stroke.
brain attack	*See* **stroke**
brain plasticity	*See* **neuroplasticity**
cerebrovascular accident (CVA)	The medical term for stroke.
coma	A prolonged state of deep unconsciousness; it may result from a stroke or be medically induced to aid healing.
computed tomography (CT) scan	A diagnostic technique in which the combined use of a computer and X-rays produces cross-sectional images of tissue. It provides clearer, more detailed information than X-rays alone.

constraint-induced movement therapy (CI or CIMT)	A stroke rehabilitation technique in which a patient's more functional limb is restrained, forcing use of the stroke-affected limb in the performance of various tasks.
diffusion-weighted imaging (DWI)	A very sensitive type of magnetic resonance imaging that measures the diffusion of water particles in brain tissue.
electroencephalogram (EEG)	A record of the tiny electrical impulses produced by the brain's activity. By measuring characteristic wave patterns, an EEG can help diagnose certain conditions of the brain.
emotional lability	Exaggerated, rapidly fluctuating emotional responses; for example, sudden uncontrollable laughing or crying.
functional magnetic resonance imaging (fMRI)	A type of specialized magnetic resonance imaging that detects changes in the flow of blood in functioning brain areas.
Glasgow Coma Scale (GCS)	A clinical tool used to assess the level of consciousness in an individual with brain injury from stroke or other causes by precisely measuring vocal response, eye opening, and motor response.
hemiparesis	Weakness affecting one entire side of the body. Patients with a stroke in their right brain hemisphere may have weakness on the left side of their body, and vice versa.
hemiplegia	Complete paralysis of one entire side of the body. Patients with a stroke in their left brain hemisphere may have paralysis on the right side of their body, and vice versa.
hemorrhagic stroke	A stroke resulting from a ruptured cerebral artery bleeding into the brain.
ischemic stroke	The most common variety of stroke, caused by a reduction in the flow of blood to brain tissue.
locked-in syndrome	A rare condition, usually arising from stroke or brain injury, in which a person is conscious but completely paralyzed and unable to speak.

magnetic resonance imaging (MRI)	A diagnostic technique that provides high-quality cross-sectional images of organs within the body without X-rays or other radiation.
minimally conscious state (MCS)	A condition of severely impaired consciousness distinct from persistent vegetative state or coma, in which a patient shows intermittent signs of consciousness.
neuroplasticity	The brain's ability to compensate and recover from injury by forming new connections between neurons.
NIH Stroke Scale	An assessment tool developed by the National Institutes of Health (NIH) to evaluate the level of impairment resulting from a stroke.
persistent vegetative state (PVS)	An ongoing condition resulting from severe brain damage (from stroke or other causes) in which the patient does not respond to physical or psychological stimuli.
positron emission tomography (PET) scan	A computerized diagnostic technique that uses radioactive substances to examine structures of the body. When used to assess the brain, it produces a three-dimensional image that reflects the brain's metabolic and chemical activity.
single-photon emission tomography (SPECT) scan	A computerized diagnostic technique that is similar to positron emission tomography. It produces lower resolution images than a PET scan but is less expensive.
stem cell	An undifferentiated, or generic, cell that can produce endless identical copies of itself as well as more specialized cells (such as brain cells).
stroke	A sudden loss of brain function resulting from an interruption of the blood supply, caused by either the blockage of a blood vessel (ischemic stroke) or the rupture of a blood vessel (hemorrhagic stroke).
tissue plasminogen activator (tPA)	A protein made in the body that dissolves blood clots. An artificially produced form is used as a medicine to treat ischemic stroke but can only be used for a few hours after symptoms appear.

transient ischemic attack (TIA)   A "mini-stroke" resulting from a temporary interruption of blood flow to an area of the brain. Symptoms last from minutes up to twenty-four hours. TIA does not cause permanent damage but is a warning sign indicating a high risk of subsequent stroke.

CHRONOLOGY

460–377 B.C.   Greek physician Hippocrates describes a medical condition in which people suddenly lose the ability to walk or speak. Because of the typically sudden and extreme nature of the symptoms, Hippocrates referred to the condition as *apoplexy*, a Greek term meaning "struck with violence." Today this condition is known as stroke. He also described cases in which right-arm paralysis was accompanied by impaired speech, possibly the first clinical description of aphasia.

A.D. 130–210   Greek physician Galen describes four symptoms often accompanying apoplexy/stroke—a loss of consciousness, changes in speech, a breathing pattern resembling that seen in deep sleep, and alterations of pulse.

1000–1450   Physicians disagree on how—or even whether—to treat stroke (at the time doctors would usually not treat patients they believed to be incurable). Treatment, if given, often consisted of bloodletting, vomiting, and purging.

1599   The term *stroke* appears in English literature for the first time, usually used by laypeople. Medical professionals continue to use the Hippocratic term *apoplexy*.

1658   During autopsies of people who died from stroke, Swiss doctor Johann Jakob Wepfer notices evidence of bleeding in the brain.

1665   Thomas Willis publishes the influential neurology work *Cerebri Anatome*, in which he describes what became known as the "circle of Willis," a network of arteries at the base of the brain. He suggests that redundancies in the network could help prevent stroke by providing alternate pathways for blood to get to the brain.

1800s   Due to the belief that overconsumption of food contributes to stroke, purging (via enemas or stimulants) is often used. Strong emotions are also believed to cause stroke, so physicians advise people to avoid overexcitement, including during sexual activity. The term *stroke* begins to be used more frequently, gradually replacing *apoplexy*.

1861   French physician Paul Broca theorizes that language function is based in a specific area of the brain (now known as Broca's area), based on the study of two patients who had language problems following damage to that brain region. He preserves the brains of the two men and donates them to the Musée Dupuytren in Paris, France.

1874   German neurologist Carl Wernicke publishes *Der Aphasische Symptomenkomple*, in which he describes an area of the brain's left hemisphere (now known as Wernicke's area) involved in understanding spoken language.

1920s–1960s   Stroke mortality rates start to decline by approximately 1 percent per year among Caucasians in the United States; among non-Caucasians the decline in mortality is much less significant over the same period.

mid-1930s   The term *cerebrovascular accident* begins to be used as a medical term for stroke.

1950   Nine out of ten stroke patients die.

1950s Surgical treatment of ischemic strokes begins to be used to open up blocked or narrowed carotid arteries.

1966 Swedish physical therapist Signe Brunnstrom describes seven stages of stroke recovery based on observation of her patients. Fred Plum and Jerome Posner define the term *locked-in syndrome*, a rare condition usually caused by a brain-stem stroke, in which a person is conscious but completely paralyzed and unable to speak.

1970s Methods of controlling hypertension (a leading cause of stroke) improve. The decline in the stroke mortality rates (in both Caucasians and non-Caucasians) accelerates. Computed tomography (CT) and magnetic resonance imaging (MRI) scanning are developed.

1972 Neurologist Fred Plum and neurosurgeon Bryan Jennett coin the term *persistent vegetative state*, describing it as a condition of "wakeful unresponsiveness" in which patients have no awareness of self or others even though their eyes are open. This condition can occur following a severe stroke.

1974 The British medical journal the *Lancet* publishes the Glasgow Coma Scale by neurosurgeon Graham Teasdale and Jennett, which becomes a standard clinical tool used to assess a patient's level of consciousness using three simple tests of verbal response, eye opening, and motor response.

1981 Neuroscientist Edward Taub develops the basis for constraint-induced movement therapy (CI) by experimenting on monkeys and prepares to begin testing the technique on human stroke patients. The organization People for the Ethical Treatment of Animals (PETA) alleges that Taub is causing needless suffering in his experimental monkeys. The animals are taken away by police, and Taub is arrested and put on trial, losing his job and his funding. Progress on CI therapy stops for several years.

1986   Having successfully defended himself against PETA's charges, Taub is hired by the University of Alabama, obtains a research grant to study strokes, and opens a clinic where he begins treating stroke patients and refining CI therapy.

1989   The American Academy of Neurology defines the term *persistent vegetative state* in a position paper, offering the opinion that such patients do not feel pain.

1990   The Decade of the Brain is declared by US president George H.W. Bush in order to foster public awareness of the importance of brain research. The Americans with Disabilities Act bans discrimination against people with disabilities; stroke is one of the main causes of long-term disability in adults.

1996   The US Food and Drug Administration (FDA) approves the first treatment for acute ischemic stroke, tissue plasminogen activator. Stroke is the second-leading organ- and disease-specific cause of death in the United States.

2000   The FDA finds that hundreds of strokes have resulted from phenylpropanolamine and orders it removed from over-the-counter cough, cold, and diet medications. The Brain Attack Coalition publishes guidelines for primary stroke centers and facilities with appropriate infrastructure and specialists in place to treat stroke patients quickly and comprehensively.

2002   The American Academy of Neurology publishes a paper distinguishing minimally conscious state (MCS) from coma and vegetative state, noting inconsistent but detectable signs of consciousness in MCS patients. The authors advise caregivers to treat the patient with dignity and be aware of the patient's potential for understanding and for perceiving pain.

2005   Age-adjusted death rates from stroke have declined by 25.4 percent compared to 1996; stroke is now the third-leading organ- and disease-specific cause of death in the United States.

2007   Neuropsychologist Nina Dronkers and a team of researchers at the University of California–Davis perform an MRI scan of the two brains preserved by Dr. Broca in 1861, creating a detailed map of the damaged areas.

2008   Fewer than one in three stroke patients die.

2010   The Centers for Disease Control and Prevention (CDC) estimate that stroke costs the United States $53.9 billion annually as a result of health care costs, medications, and missed work days. In Glasgow, Scotland, the company ReNeuron starts the first regulated trial of a neural fetal stem cell treatment for stroke-related disability, injecting stem cells from a fetus aborted in California in 2003 into the brain of an ischemic stroke patient.

2011   Israeli scientists create an artificial rat cerebellum (a brain structure regulating movement), demonstrating that artificial brain structures might someday restore function to stroke patients. The *New England Journal of Medicine* reports that patients treated with stenting (a surgical procedure) to prevent stroke fared significantly worse than those given intensive medical intervention to control risk factors.

2012   A study is published in the journal *Stem Cells* showing recovery of up to 83 percent of sensorimotor function in rats with stroke damage in the striatial brain region after an injection of ReNeuron neural stem cells.

ORGANIZATIONS TO CONTACT

The editors have compiled the following list of organizations concerned with the issues debated in this book. The descriptions are derived from materials provided by the organizations. All have publications or information available for interested readers. The list was compiled on the date of publication of the present volume; the information provided here may change. Be aware that many organizations take several weeks or longer to respond to inquiries, so allow as much time as possible.

American Academy of Neurology (AAN)
1080 Montreal Ave.,
Saint Paul, MN 55116
(800) 879-1960
fax: (651) 695-2791
e-mail: memberservices @aan.com
website: www.aan.com

Established in 1948, the AAN is an international professional association of more than twenty-one thousand neurologists and neuroscience professionals who care for patients with neurological disorders. The academy publishes the *Neurology Journal* and the biweekly newsletter *Neurology Today*. Its website offers a searchable archive of fact sheets, news articles, and research summaries, including "Why Are People with Stroke More Likely to Die if Hospitalized on Weekend?" and "Telestroke System Extends Expert Stroke Care into Rural Areas."

American Association of Neurological Surgeons (AANS)
5550 Meadowbrook Dr., Rolling Meadows, IL 60008
(888) 566-2267
fax: (847) 378-0600
e-mail: info@aans.org
website: www.aans.org

Representing doctors who specialize in brain surgery, the AANS promotes neurosurgery as a science and publishes the *Journal of Neurosurgery*, which contains articles outlining the latest advances in brain surgery. Visitors to the website can find statistics about neurosurgery, press releases outlining the society's efforts to advance the science of neurosurgery, and news reports about stroke, such as "Neurosurgeons Report That Prevention and Quick Treatment Are Keys to Effective Stroke Treatment" and "Trends in Cost and Outcome of Hospitalization for Stroke and Stroke Subtypes in the United States Over the Last Decade." The website also features a "Patient Information" page, with a section on stroke and related conditions.

American Stroke Association (ASA)
7272 Greenville Ave.,
Dallas, TX 75231
(888) 478-7653
website: www.stroke
association.org

The ASA was created in 1997 with the goal of saving lives from stroke through better prevention, diagnosis, and treatment. The organization funds scientific research, provides information to the public, and guides health care professionals to better manage stroke. It publishes *Stroke Connection* magazine in both print and e-zine formats.

Centers for Disease Control and Prevention (CDC)
1600 Clifton Rd.,
Atlanta, GA 30333
(800) 232-4636
e-mail: cdcinfo@cdc.gov
website: www.cdc.gov

As the federal government's chief public health agency, the CDC explores trends in diseases and other conditions that affect the health of Americans. The National Center for Injury Prevention and Control, an agency of the CDC, maintains an extensive archive of information on stroke, which includes statistics, educational materials such as fact sheets and podcasts, and links to journal articles and abstracts.

Heart and Stroke Foundation of Canada
222 Queen St., Ste.
1402, Ottawa, ON
K1P 5V9
(613) 569-4361
fax: (613) 569-3278
website: www.heartand
stroke.com

The Heart and Stroke Foundation is a health charity based in Canada that is made up of ten provincial foundations and supported by more than 130,000 volunteers. Its goals include the promotion of healthy living, advancing stroke research and its application, and advocating on behalf of stroke patients. The organization's website offers a wealth of information in English and French, as well as a "Multicultural Resources" section that includes information for those of African, First Nations, Inuit, Métis, Chinese, South Asian, and Persian/Iranian descent. A free monthly e-newsletter, *Heart & Stroke He@lthline*, is also available through the website.

National Institute of Mental Health (NIMH)
6001 Executive Blvd.,
Bethesda, MD 20892
(866) 615-6464
e-mail: nimhinfo@nih
.gov
website: www.nimh.
nih.gov

The NIMH is the federal government's chief funding agency for mental health research in America. The organization's website offers a wealth of information on the brain; of particular note is the section on "Depression and Stroke," which includes sections such as "What Is Depression?," "What Is a Stroke?," "How Are Depression and Stroke Linked?," and "How Is Depression Treated in People Who Have Had a Stroke?"

National Institute of Neurological Disorders and Stroke (NINDS)
PO Box 5801,
Bethesda, MD 20824
(800) 352-9424
website: www.ninds
.nih.gov

The NINDS is an agency of the National Institutes of Health. The organization's mission is to reduce the burden of neurological disease, including stroke and brain injury. To this end, it conducts, fosters, coordinates, and guides research on the causes, prevention, diagnosis, and treatment of neurological disease and supports basic research in related scientific areas. Visitors to the agency's website can find a description of stroke, an explanation of methods of treatment and rehabilitation, and the status of research into the causes and treatment of stroke.

National Stroke Association
9707 E. Easter Ln.,
Ste. B, Centennial, CO
80112
(800) 787-6537
e-mail: info@stroke
.org
website: www.stroke
.org

The mission of the National Stroke Association is to reduce the incidence and impact of stroke by developing compelling education and programs focused on prevention, treatment, rehabilitation, and support for all impacted by stroke. Its website offers the quarterly magazine *StrokeSmart*, the bimonthly *Brain Alert Newsletter*, fact sheets, and brochures. Some information is available in Spanish, and there is a section on African Americans and stroke.

Stroke Association
Stroke House, 240
City Rd., London,
EC1V 2PR
(020) 7566-0300
fax: (020) 7490-2686
text: (020) 7251-9096
e-mail: info@stroke
.org.uk
website: www.stroke
.org.uk

The Stroke Association is a United Kingdom–based charitable organization solely concerned with combating stroke in people of all ages. It funds research into prevention, treatment, and better methods of rehabilitation and helps stroke patients and their families directly through its Life After Stroke services, which include information, advice and support, communication support, and Life After Stroke grants. The organization produces a number of publications, including patient leaflets, the quarterly magazine *Stroke News*, and information for health professionals. It also hosts the online community forum Talk-Stroke, which can be accessed through its website.

US Food and Drug Administration (FDA)
10903 New
Hampshire Ave.,
Silver Spring, MD
20993
(888) 463-6332
website: www.fda.gov

An arm of the US Department of Health and Human Services, the FDA is responsible for assuring the safety, efficacy, and security of human and veterinary drugs, medical devices, and the food supply. The FDA is also responsible for advancing pubic health by helping to speed innovations that make medicines more effective, safer, and more affordable and for helping the public get the science-based information they need regarding medicines and foods in order to maintain and improve their health. The searchable A–Z index at its website includes health articles and news releases, such as "FDA Approves Xarelto to Prevent Stroke in People with Common Type of Abnormal Heart Rhythm" and "Aspirin for Reducing Your Risk of Heart Attack and Stroke: Know the Facts."

FOR FURTHER READING

Books   Diane Ackerman, *One Hundred Names for Love: A Stroke, a Marriage, and the Language of Healing.* New York: Norton, 2011.

Jean-Dominique Bauby, *The Diving Bell and the Butterfly: A Memoir of Life in Death.* New York: Vintage, 2007.

Kip Burkman, *The Stroke Recovery Book: A Guide for Patients and Families.* 2nd ed. Omaha, NE: Addicas, 2010.

Norman Doidge, *The Brain That Changes Itself.* New York: Viking, 2007.

Howard Engel, *The Man Who Forgot How to Read.* New York: St. Martin's, 2008.

Candis Fancher, Lindsey McDivitt, and Jacquelyn B. Fletcher, *Climbing the Mountain: Stories of Hope and Healing After Stroke and Brain Injury.* Minneapolis: Fairview, 2008.

Kinan K. Hreib, *100 Questions and Answers About Stroke: A Lahey Clinic Guide.* Sudbury, MA: Jones and Bartlett, 2009.

Mark McEwen and Daniel Paisner, *Change in the Weather: Life After Stroke.* New York: Gotham, 2008.

Amy Ellis Nutt, *Shadows Bright as Glass: The Remarkable Story of One Man's Journey from Brain Trauma to Artistic Triumph.* New York: Free Press, 2011.

Oliver Sacks, *The Mind's Eye.* New York: Knopf, 2010.

Alison Bonds Shapiro, *Healing into Possibility: The Transformational Lessons of a Stroke.* Tiburon, CA: Kramer, 2009.

Jill Bolte Taylor, *My Stroke of Insight: A Brain Scientist's Personal Journey.* New York: Viking, 2008.

Paul West, *The Shadow Factory.* Santa Fe, NM: Lumen, 2008.

Olajide Williams, *Stroke Diaries: A Guide for Survivors and Their Families*. New York: Oxford University Press, 2010.

Justin A. Zivin and John Simmons, *TPA for Stroke: The Story of a Controversial Drug*. New York: Oxford University Press, 2011.

Periodicals and Internet Sources

Peter Applebome, "Losing Movement, but Not Wisdom or Love," *New York Times*, December 16, 2007.

Sherry Baker, "The Rise of the Cyborgs: Melding Humans and Machines to Help the Paralyzed Walk, the Mute Speak, and the Near-Dead Return to Life," *Discover*, October 2008. http://discover magazine.com/2008/oct/26-rise-of-the-cyborgs/article_view?b _start:int:=0.

Dakshana Bascaramurty, "Who Says Stroke Rehabilitation Can't Be Fun?," *Globe and Mail* (Toronto), June 14, 2010.

Bruce Bower, "Self-Serve Brains: Personal Identity Veers to the Right Hemisphere," *Science News*, February 11, 2006. http://bio psychiatry.com/misc/personal-identity.html.

Andreas von Bubnoff, "Brain Attack: Progress Is Slow in Finding Better Ischemic-Stroke Therapies," *Science News*, July 14, 2007.

Fiona Campbell and David Gillespie, "Effect of Stroke on Family Carers and Family Relationships," *Nursing Standard*, vol. 26, no. 2, 2011.

Caroline Cassels, "Misdiagnosis of Young Stroke Patients Not Uncommon," Medscape Medical News, February 19, 2009. www.medscape.com/viewarticle/588453.

Jonathan Dienst, "Children Don't Have Strokes? Just Ask Jared," *New York Times*, January 19, 2010. www.nytimes.com /2010/01/19/health/19stroke.html?pagewanted=all.

Pallab Ghosh, "UK Stem Cell Stroke Trial Passes First Safety Test," BBC News, September 1, 2011. www.bbc.co.uk/news /health-14731682.

Kristina Grifantini, "Robo-Rehab at Home," *Technology Review*, November 13, 2009. www.technologyreview.com/computing /23939.

Harriet Hall, "Thoughts on Neuroplasticity," *Science-Based Medicine* (blog), March 18, 2008. www.sciencebasedmedicine .org/index.php/thoughts-on-neuroplasticity.

Virginia Hughes, "Breaking Through," *Last Word on Nothing* (blog), November 29, 2011. www.lastwordonnothing.com /2011/11/29/breaking-through.

Robert Krulwich, "The Writer Who Couldn't Read," *Krulwich Wonders* (blog), NPR, June 21, 2010. www.npr.org/blogs/krul wich/2011/06/01/127745750/the-writer-who-couldnt-read.

Tan Ee Lyn, "Patients Pay with Their Lives for Unproven Stem Cell Therapies," *Taipei Times*, September 26, 2011. www.taipei times.com/News/editorials/archives/2011/09/26/2003514195/1.

Kat McGowan, "Rediscovering Consciousness in People Diagnosed as 'Vegetative,'" *Discover*, July 6, 2011. http://discover magazine.com/2011/mar/09-turning-vegetables-back-into-humans.

Marci Lee Nilsen, "A Historical Account of Stroke and the Evolution of Nursing Care for Stroke Patients," *Journal of Neuroscience Nursing*, February 2010.

Nina, "My Post-Stroke Depression," *Embracing Recovery . . . My New Life* (blog), September 7, 2011. http://ninasstrokestory .blogspot.com/2011/09/my-post-stroke-depression.html.

Steven Novella, "Communicating with the Locked-In," *Science-Based Medicine* (blog), December 16, 2009. www.sciencebased medicine.org/index.php/communicating-with-the-locked-in.

George P. Prigatano, "The Importance of the Patient's Subjective Experience in Stroke Rehabilitation," *Topics in Stroke Rehabilitation*, vol. 18, no. 1, 2011.

Scientific American, "Better Brains: The Revolution in Brain Science," August 8, 2007. www.scientificamerican.com/podcast /episode.cfm?id=465B1677-E7F2-99DF-36E1378B1640D492.

Michael E. Selzer, "Harnessing the Brain's Power to Adapt After Injury," Dana Foundation, November 6, 2007. www.dana.org /news/cerebrum/detail.aspx?id=9996.

Alison Bonds Shapiro, "A Story to Create: Stroke Survivors' Broken Narratives," *Topics in Stroke Rehabilitation*, vol. 18, no. 1, 2011.

Matthew Shulman, "Music as Medicine for the Brain," *U.S. News Health,* July 17, 2008. http://health.usnews.com/health-news/family-health/brain-and-behavior/articles/2008/07/17/music-as-medicine-for-the-brain.

Scott Silliman, "A Neurologist's Perspective," *ASHA Leader,* April 17, 2007. www.asha.org/Publications/leader/2007/070417/f070417a3.htm.

Emily Singer, "Repairing the Stroke-Damaged Brain," *Technology Review*, June 24, 2009. www.technologyreview.com/biomedicine/22921.

Donna Smith, "If You Had a Stroke Tomorrow, Where Would You End Up? Why We Need Medicare for All," AlterNet, July 7, 2011. www.alternet.org/story/151557/if_you_had_a_stroke_tomorrow,_where_would_you_end_up_why_we_need_medicare_for_all._?page=entire.

Nona Stuck, "Fighting My Health Fate," *Prevention*, July 2009.

Robert Teasell, "'Holistic' Care for Stroke in the Context of the Current Health Care Bureaucracy and Economic Reality," *Topics in Stroke Rehabilitation*, vol. 18, no. 1, 2011.

Chris Woolston, "Women and Stroke Risk: Tangled Truth About Your Health," *Prevention*, November 2011. www.prevention.com/health/health-concerns/women-and-stroke-risk.

INDEX